THE EVERYTHING®
LARGE-PRINT CRYPTOGRAMS BOOK
VOLUME II

Dear Reader,

Do you like solving word puzzles and cryptograms? Do you enjoy reading quotations from your favorite athletes, politicians, and entertainers? If so, you'll love this book!

I wrote *The Everything® Large-Print Cryptograms Book, Volume II* to serve as your escape from time-consuming everyday tasks. Sometimes it's fun to sit down, solve a cryptogram, and find an interesting quotation that you can ponder as you complete your day.

In this book you will find cryptograms on many different topics that we encounter in everyday life. Each puzzle's solution contains a quotation or maxim that relates to that chapter's topic or theme. Some of the puzzles will be easy to solve, while others will give you a chance to maximize your brainpower! If you do get stuck, each cryptogram has a clue at the end of each chapter to assist you.

XJIU POL (Have fun)!
Nikki Katz

Nikki Katz

Welcome to the EVERYTHING® Series!

These handy, accessible books give you all you need to tackle a difficult project, gain a new hobby, comprehend a fascinating topic, prepare for an exam, or even brush up on something you learned back in school but have since forgotten.

You can choose to read an *Everything*® book from cover to cover or just pick out the information you want from our four useful boxes: e-questions, e-facts, e-alerts, and e-ssentials. We give you everything you need to know on the subject, but throw in a lot of fun stuff along the way, too.

We now have more than 400 *Everything*® books in print, spanning such wide-ranging categories as weddings, pregnancy, cooking, music instruction, foreign language, crafts, pets, New Age, and so much more. When you're done reading them all, you can finally say you know *Everything*®!

PUBLISHER Karen Cooper

DIRECTOR OF ACQUISITIONS AND INNOVATION Paula Munier

MANAGING EDITOR, EVERYTHING® SERIES Lisa Laing

COPY CHIEF Casey Ebert

ACQUISITIONS EDITOR Lisa Laing

EDITORIAL ASSISTANT Ross Weisman

EVERYTHING® SERIES COVER DESIGNER Erin Alexander

LAYOUT DESIGNERS Colleen Cunningham, Elisabeth Lariviere, Ashley Vierra, Denise Wallace

Visit the entire Everything® series at *www.everything.com*

THE EVERYTHING®

LARGE-PRINT CRYPTOGRAMS BOOK
VOLUME II

Challenge your brain without
straining your eyes!

Nikki Katz

Avon, Massachusetts

Dedication

To my family

———

Published by
Adams Media, a division of F+W Media, Inc.
57 Littlefield Street, Avon, MA 02322. U.S.A.
www.adamsmedia.com

Contains material adapted and abridged from *The Everything*®
Cryptograms Book, by Nikki Katz, copyright © 2005 by F+W
Media, Inc., ISBN 10: 1-59337-319-8, ISBN 13: 978-1-59337-319-1.

ISBN 10: 1-4405-1022-9
ISBN 13: 978-1-4405-1022-9
eISBN 10: 1-4405-1023-7
eISBN 13: 978-1-4405-1023-6

Printed in the United States of America.

10 9 8 7 6 5 4 3 2 1

Some additional information adapted from *The Everything® Word Games Challenge Book*, by Charles Timmerman, copyright © 2005 by F+W Media, Inc., ISBN 10: 1-59337-312-0, ISBN 13: 978-1-59337-312-2.

This book is available at quantity discounts for bulk purchases. For information, please call 1-800-289-09632.

Acknowledgments

Thank you again to my agent, Barb Doyen at Doyen and Doyen Literary Services Inc., and to the multiple editors I worked with at Adams Media—including Kate McBride, Gina Chaimanis, and Julie Gutin.

I would also like to thank my husband, Jason, and my children—Katelyn, Kendall, and Lincoln. Their support is fundamental in allowing me to take time to write; time that is, in essence, away from them.

Contents

Introduction

ARE YOU GETTING bored with trying to find quality crossword puzzles and solving them quickly? Are you still searching for someone to join you in playing a game of hangman or Scrabble? Or are you just looking for a new way to pass the time on your next airplane trip or daily commute? If you answered "yes" to any of these questions, then this book is perfect for you. Cryptograms are a form of word games that offer a way to challenge your brain by allowing you to solve puzzles and codes. This second volume of cryptograms contains puzzles that will allow you to test your memory of a wide variety of quotations on a range of topics. These cryptograms are fun for both the novice and the expert, offering both simpler, lengthier puzzles with more language clues for you to decipher as well as more challenging puzzles with shorter and more obscure quotations.

Almost everyone has used codes to hide information at some point in his or her life. Perhaps you wrote and deciphered secret messages with your friends in a code you all carried the solution to in your pockets when you were a child. Or maybe you wrote in your journal in a code so that your parents and teachers could not understand it. You might have talked in pig Latin to your friends in the hopes that others would not know what you were saying. Or it's possible you drew pictures that incorporated a code or various images that only the recipient would understand. But even if you did not use codes in these situations, you have probably read or spoken acronyms and abbreviations, which are actually codes as well! These common language tricks are a method of shortening a longer word or phrase but, when you speak or hear them, you understand the complete meaning behind the shortened variation.

The Everything® Large-Print Cryptograms Book, Volume II is a great resource for practicing your code-solving skills as it teaches you exactly what cryptograms are, provides tips for solving them, and offers multiple chapters of cryptogram puzzles to practice your skills with plenty of room to work. If you get stuck on any particular puzzle, make sure to check the end of each chapter for a hint word (but try to avoid looking in the Appendix for the answers).

Please note that as you are solving the puzzles you may find that a coded letter (or two) in a particular puzzle is the same as the uncoded letter within the solution. This is not an attempt to trick you or throw you off but rather is just the nature of cryptograms.

If you're ready to start enjoying this book, those new to cryptograms or in need of a quick refresher should head to Chapter 1. Those confident in their puzzle-solving abilities can skip to any of the other chapters to start solving puzzles in a topic of interest to you!

CHAPTER 1

Cryptograms 101

Cryptograms are fun word puzzles that involve phrases and text that have been converted into code. When you solve a cryptogram, you have to figure these codes out yourself based on your knowledge of the English language. This chapter provides basic terminology to get you started, a quick history of cryptograms, general tips for solving the puzzles, and an sample solution.

BASIC TERMINOLOGY

There are many different terms used in the cryptographic lexicon, and you'll learn their meanings here. To begin, the message that will be coded is written originally in what is called plaintext or cleartext. The act of encoding that message to hide its contents from other readers is called *encryption*. Once a message has been encrypted, it is called either a *cryptogram* or *ciphertext*. The act of decoding the message and turning the ciphertext back into plaintext is called decryption. The key, if available, explains the code and is used to decrypt the ciphertext.

The science of cryptograms is called *cryptography* and the people who study it are called *cryptographers*. The act of breaking a cipher without knowing the key is known as *cryptanalysis*, and the people who perform cryptanalyses are *cryptanalysts*.

A *cipher* is a cryptographic system or method of encryption and decryption. A *transposition cipher* is one where the letters in the original plaintext are rearranged within the original message. The entire message could be written backwards, each word could be written backwards, or the letters could be scrambled. In a *substitution cipher*, each letter of the plaintext is replaced with another letter or symbol. In a simple substitution, each letter of the plaintext is always replaced with the same letter or symbol. No other letters use that symbol, so there is a one-to-one relationship in the key. In a *polyalphabetic substitution cipher*, two or more cipher alphabets are used to make the encryption more secure.

HISTORY OF CRYPTOLOGY

The history of cryptology dates back to approximately 1900 B.C. It was discovered then that an Egyptian scribe used nonstandard hieroglyphics in his communication. As the years progressed, cryptology was used in other parts of the world. For instance, history teaches us that a Mesopotamian tablet recorded an encrypted recipe for making glazes for pottery around 1500 B.C. In approximately 500 B.C., Hebrew scribes used the Atbash Cipher to write the book of Jeremiah. Spartans used a "scytale" cipher device to communicate between military commanders around 400 B.C., and sometime between 50 and 60 B.C. the Caesar Cipher was created by Julius Caesar to communicate with his army.

As civilization moved forward, so did the understanding and use of cryptology. The Arabs used both substitution and transposition ciphers, and by approximately 1412 A.D. al-Kalka-shandi included several cryptographic systems in his encyclopedia. The Europeans began using cryptography in the Middle Ages, often substituting only the vowels within their plaintext. A cryptography manual was published around 1379 by Gabriele de Lavinde of Parma, who served Pope Clement VII. The Rosetta Stone, found in Egypt in 1799, was used to decipher hieroglyphics from around 200 B.C., translating the same message into both Greek and Egyptian.

During the last few centuries, cryptograms have become extremely useful in times of war as they can cloak all manner of communications. In the American Civil War, for instance, the Federal army used transposition ciphers for their communications while the Confederate army used the Vigenère Cipher, which the Union army could typically solve. In World Wars I and II, all military operations were using cryptography. The German army used the Enigma machine to create "unbreakable" codes for their radio messages. Fortunately, both British and American codebreakers were actually able to crack this code and make a substantial contribution to the Allied war effort.

The field of cryptography remained a well-kept secret, one often misunderstood even by those who knew about it, until computers became more popular and more affordable to the general public. The demand for encryption increased thanks to our desire to communicate digitally. In 1977, the National Bureau of Standards published the Data Encryption Standard (DES) to be used by government agencies and banks. That same year, Ron

Rivest, Adi Shamir, and Leonard Adleman developed an algorithm for Internet encryption and authentication, known as RSA, that is still used today. This algorithm is included in the Netscape and Internet Explorer browsers.

FAMOUS CIPHERS

There are quite a few well-known historical ciphers that are still used by people today to code simple messages. These codes include the Caesar Cipher, the Atbash Cipher, and the Vigenère Cipher, all of which are described in detail below.

Caesar Cipher

It's a simple matter to encrypt and decrypt messages using the Caesar Cipher because the plaintext letters are replaced by ciphertext letters that are three places down the alphabet: The letter A is replaced with the letter D, the letter B is replaced with the letter E, and so on.

Caesar Cipher

A	B	C	D	E	F	G	H	I	J	K	L	M	N
D	E	F	G	H	I	J	K	L	M	N	O	P	Q
O	P	Q	R	S	T	U	V	W	X	Y	Z		
R	S	T	U	V	W	X	Y	Z	A	B	C		

Atbash Cipher

The Atbash Cipher is another straightforward substitution code, and one of the few ciphers to use the Hebrew language. The Hebrew word "atbash" actually explains the substitution method used. The first letter, aleph, is followed by the last letter, tav. The second letter, beth, is followed by the second to last letter, shin. In using the Atbash Cipher for the English language, A is replaced by Z, B is replaced by Y, and so on.

Atbash Cipher

A	B	C	D	E	F	G	H	I	J	K	L	M	N
Z	Y	X	W	V	U	T	S	R	Q	P	O	N	M
O	P	Q	R	S	T	U	V	W	X	Y	Z		
L	K	J	I	H	G	F	E	D	C	B	A		

Vigenère Cipher

The Vigenère Cipher was created by Blaise de Vigenère, a member of the court of French king Henry III during the sixteenth century. This cipher is a polyalphabetic substitution cipher requiring the following table and a keyword, where the keyword is a random word used to help encrypt the message.

Vigenere Cipher

	A	B	C	D	E	F	G	H	I	J	K	L
A:	A	B	C	D	E	F	G	H	I	J	K	L
B:	B	C	D	E	F	G	H	I	J	K	L	M
C:	C	D	E	F	G	H	I	J	K	L	M	N
D:	D	E	F	G	H	I	J	K	L	M	N	O
E:	E	F	G	H	I	J	K	L	M	N	O	P
F:	F	G	H	I	J	K	L	M	N	O	P	Q
G:	G	H	I	J	K	L	M	N	O	P	Q	R
H:	H	I	J	K	L	M	N	O	P	Q	R	S
I:	I	J	K	L	M	N	O	P	Q	R	S	T
J:	J	K	L	M	N	O	P	Q	R	S	T	U
K:	K	L	M	N	O	P	Q	R	S	T	U	V
L:	L	M	N	O	P	Q	R	S	T	U	V	W
M:	M	N	O	P	Q	R	S	T	U	V	W	X

M	**N**	**O**	**P**	**Q**	**R**	**S**	**T**	**U**	**V**	**W**	**X**	**Y**	**Z**
M	N	O	P	Q	R	S	T	U	V	W	X	Y	Z
N	O	P	Q	R	S	T	U	V	W	X	Y	Z	A
O	P	Q	R	S	T	U	V	W	X	Y	Z	A	B
P	Q	R	S	T	U	V	W	X	Y	Z	A	B	C
Q	R	S	T	U	V	W	X	Y	Z	A	B	C	D
R	S	T	U	V	W	X	Y	Z	A	B	C	D	E
S	T	U	V	W	X	Y	Z	A	B	C	D	E	F
T	U	V	W	X	Y	Z	A	B	C	D	E	F	G
U	V	W	X	Y	Z	A	B	C	D	E	F	G	H
V	W	X	Y	Z	A	B	C	D	E	F	G	H	I
W	X	Y	Z	A	B	C	D	E	F	G	H	I	J
X	Y	Z	A	B	C	D	E	F	G	H	I	J	K
Y	Z	A	B	C	D	E	F	G	H	I	J	K	L

Vigenere Cipher (continued)

	A	B	C	D	E	F	G	H	I	J	K	L
N:	N	O	P	Q	R	S	T	U	V	W	X	Y
O:	O	P	Q	R	S	T	U	V	W	X	Y	Z
P:	P	Q	R	S	T	U	V	W	X	Y	Z	A
Q:	Q	R	S	T	U	V	W	X	Y	Z	A	B
R:	R	S	T	U	V	W	X	Y	Z	A	B	C
S:	S	T	U	V	W	X	Y	Z	A	B	C	D
T:	T	U	V	W	X	Y	Z	A	B	C	D	E
U:	U	V	W	X	Y	Z	A	B	C	D	E	F
V:	V	W	X	Y	Z	A	B	C	D	E	F	G
W:	W	X	Y	Z	A	B	C	D	E	F	G	H
X:	X	Y	Z	A	B	C	D	E	F	G	H	I
Y:	Y	Z	A	B	C	D	E	F	G	H	I	J
Z:	Z	A	B	C	D	E	F	G	H	I	J	K

M N O P Q R S T U V W X Y Z

Z A B C D E F G H I J K L M
A B C D E F G H I J K L M N
B C D E F G H I J K L M N O
C D E F G H I J K L M N O P
D E F G H I J K L M N O P Q
E F G H I J K L M N O P Q R
F G H I J K L M N O P Q R S
G H I J K L M N O P Q R S T
H I J K L M N O P Q R S T U
I J K L M N O P Q R S T U V
J K L M N O P Q R S T U V W
K L M N O P Q R S T U V W X
L M N O P Q R S T U V W X Y

Let's say you wished to encrypt the phrase LOVE ALL, TRUST A FEW, DO WRONG TO NONE using the keyword TURNIP. You would start off by writing the word TURNIP above the phrase as many times as it takes to complete it. Then to determine the ciphertext, use the letter at the intersection of the row using the keyword letter and the column using the phrase letter.

You need the keyword to decrypt the message, even if you're given the ciphertext. You would write the keyword multiple times over the ciphertext and then use a Vigenère square to look up the row of the keyword letter. Once you found the letter, you'd follow along the row until you found the ciphertext letter, and follow that up the column to find the corresponding plaintext solution.

UNSOLVED CRYPTOGRAMS

Not all cryptograms are easy to solve, and in fact there are many famous unsolved codes and ciphers. The Voynich manuscript is a nearly 235-page document written entirely in a strange, unknown alphabet. The manuscript is over 400 years old, and has yet to be decoded.

Another unsolved cipher was sent on July 14, 1897, by composer Edward Elgar. He sent a letter to a friend of his, Dora Penny, written completely in code. She was unable to read the letter, and he never explained it. Miss Penny attempted to have other people solve it, but to this day the code has not been cracked.

Archaeologist Sir Arthur Evans uncovered clay tablets with mysterious symbols in Crete in 1900. He spent a great amount of time attempting to decrypt the three different writing systems used (a hieroglyphic script, and two systems later referred to as Linear A and Linear B). To this day, only Linear B has been solved.

In the late 1960s, a serial killer nicknamed the Zodiac Killer sent multiple coded communications to the police and editors of publications. Some of those letters were solved, but many were not.

The famous Edgar Allan Poe Cryptographic Challenge that was only just recently solved. Poe was enthralled with cryptography and challenged his readers to send him cryptograms to solve. A "Mr. W. B. Tyler" submitted two cryptograms to Poe, who never found solutions for them. Instead he challenged his audience to solve them. It has been speculated that perhaps Poe created the cryptograms himself, but nobody has been able to prove it. It wasn't until 150 years later that Gil Broza of Toronto cracked the cipher.

TIPS FOR SOLVING CRYPTOGRAMS

Now that you know what a cryptogram is, it's time to give you some tips for solving the type you'll see here. The puzzles in this book use simple substitutions to encrypt the quotations you'll be trying to solve. Each letter will be replaced by a different letter, but the original spacing and punctuation will remain in place. Since you will not be given the key, your job is to decipher the puzzle using the topic given and your knowledge of the English language.

Common Letters and Words

In English, E is the most common letter, followed by T, A, O, N, I, and R, in that order. The words A and I are the most common one-letter words, with O coming in at a very distant third place. The most common two-letter words are OF, TO, IN, IS, IT, BE, BY, HE, AS, ON, AT, OR, AN, SO, IF, and NO. The most common three-letter words are THE and AND, followed by FOR, HIS, NOT, BUT, YOU, ARE, HER, and HAD. The most common four-letter word is THAT, followed by WITH, HAVE, and FROM. If you see a four-letter word that begins and ends in the same letter, you might want to try "that" first.

The letter Q is almost always followed by U, while E is the most common letter at the end of a word. T is the most common letter at the beginning of a word. If there is an apostrophe in the puzzle, it means that the word is either possessive (John's) or it is a contraction (won't). If a single letter follows the apostrophe, it's usually an S or a T and, if the letter is a T, the letter before the apostrophe is an N.

Don't Forget the Vowels

When it comes to vowels, the majority of two-letter words start with an A, I, O, or U or end with an E, O, or Y. The letters O and E are often seen in double letters, whereas the other vowels are rarely seen. The letter A is usually seen as the initial letter in a word or the second letter from the end. More often than not, the letter E is the second letter in a word or the final letter, but that doesn't mean it won't also be scattered throughout words.

The letter I is most often seen as the third letter from the end (ION and ING being common endings). The letter O is usually seen as the second letter in a word or the final letter. The letter U is typically seen as the first letter in a word or the second letter from the end. The letter Y is usually the last letter in a word.

Where Do I Start?

Solving cryptograms involves a lot of trial and error. You may want to start out by counting the letters and remembering that the most common letter is an E. Although this often gives you a good jump start, there may be a few puzzles that have no Es at all. Knowing one or two letters of a word can often help you solve the rest of that word, even as it gives you letters sprinkled throughout other words in the puzzle. Words that commonly go together, like "it is," can be helpful as well. Contrary to what you might think, longer cryptograms are easier to solve than shorter ones because they offer more instances of letters and patterns for you to view.

FOR EXAMPLE

Now that you've seen some tips for solving cryptograms, here is an example and the corresponding solution. You'll be solving the following cryptogram:

GQP XBHHPEPDFP APGIPPD GQP EBTQG INEX KDX GQP KCUNJG EBTQG INEX BJ GQP XBHHPEPDFP APGIPPD CBTQGDBDT KDX K CBTQGDBDT AVT. —UKEZ GIKBD

A good first step is to count the letters and see which occurs most often. In this case, it's the letter P, which probably means that it represents the letter E.

Letter Count

A	B	C	D	E	F	G	H	I	J	K	L	M	N
3	10	3	11	7	2	12	4	5	2	6	0	0	3

O	P	Q	R	S	T	U	V	W	X	Y	Z
0	16	8	0	0	7	2	1	0	6	0	1

If you look for the most common three-letter word in the puzzle you will see that GQP occurs four times, so that combination is most likely the word THE. Since you've already speculated that P is E, your guess is probably correct. Therefore, you can now go into the puzzle and substitute E for P, T for G, and H for Q.

The puzzle now looks like this:

the XBHHeEeDFe AetleeD the EBTht INEX KDX the KCUNJt EBTht INEX BJ the XBHHeEeDFe AetleeD CBThtDBDT KDX K CBThtDBDT AVT.
—UKEZ tIKBD

If you now look at the second most common three-letter word, you will see that KDX occurs twice. You'll also see that K appears as a single letter one time. This probably signifies that K is A, and therefore KDX is AND. Thanks to this process of elimination, you can substitute A for K, N for D, and D for X:

the dBHHeEenFe Aetleen the EBTht INEd and the aCUNJt EBTht INEd BJ the dBHHeEenFe Aetleen CBThtnBnT and a CBThtnBnT AVT.
—UaEZ tIaBn

Looking at Aetleen, you can speculate that the word is BETWEEN, so A becomes B and I becomes W:

the dBHHeEenFe between the EBTht wNEd and the aCUNJt EBTht wNEd BJ the dBHHeEenFe between CBThtnBnT and a CBThtnBnT bVT.
—UaEZ twaBn

You can tell from how the letters fall in the word dBHHeEenFe and from the context of the sentence that the word is DIFFER-ENCE, so B becomes I, H becomes F, E becomes R, and F becomes C:

the difference between the riTht wNrd and the aCUNJt riTht wNrd iJ the difference between CiThtninT and a CiThtninT bVT.
—UarZ twaIn

If you look at the word CiThtninT, you can speculate that the T would need to be a G, making the word Cightning. The next obvious logical conclusion is that C would become an L for lightning:

the difference between the right wNrd and the alUNJt right wNrd iJ the difference between lightning and a lightning bVg.
—UarZ twain

When you look at iJ, you know it has to be either it, is, or in. Since T and N are already accounted for, the word must be is, and so the letter S can be substituted for any Js:

the difference between the right wNrd and the alUNst right wNrd is the difference between lightning and a lightning bVg.
—UarZ twain

If you look at words bVg and wNrd, you see that V and N need to be vowels. The only two vowels left are O and U, so the V is a U for "bug" and the N is an O for "word."

the difference between the right word and the alUost right word is the difference between lightning and a lightning bug.
—UarZ twain

Now, it's easy to see that alUost is "almost," so the U in this code stands for M. You can now probably guess that the author of this quote is Mark Twain, so the Z becomes a K. The solved puzzle is:

The difference between the right word and the almost right word is the difference between lightning and a lightning bug.
—Mark Twain

Example Cryptogram: Reference Code

A	B	C	D	E	F	G	H	I	J	K	L	M	N
K	A	F	X	P	H	T	Q	B	R	Z	C	U	D
O	P	Q	R	S	T	U	V	W	X	Y	Z
N	Y	L	E	J	G	V	O	I	S	M	W

CHAPTER 2

Holiday Celebrations

What is a holiday without some traditional songs, remarkable quotations, funny sayings, and serious expressions? After all, Christmas just wouldn't be Christmas without some caroling! So take a short holiday, or just a little break in your day, and solve these cryptograms involving birthdays, Christmas, Thanksgiving, New Year's, and Halloween. Some of the quotations are fun and silly, while others are more serious and will leave you with something to ponder.

HAPPY BIRTHDAY

Puzzle 2-1 *answers on page 236*

I QNEKBJIZ NV I JIT MLB IKMIDV AHJHJUHAV

_____

I MBJIT'V UNAZLQID UYZ THRHA

_____

AHJHJUHAV LHA IPH.

_____

—ABUHAZ OABVZ _____

Puzzle 2-2 *answers on page 236*

HPRDYOITB IRA NJJO EJR TJC. B DIDPB

_____

DPMB BYJW DYID DYA KAJKZA WYJ YIUA

_____

DYA XJBD ZPUA DYA ZJLNABD.

_____

—ZIRRT ZJRALVJLP _____

Puzzle 2-3 *answers on page 236*

SGQE AJSLDTQZO QSG RCL QR

_____

RMQE QNNQJSO. SGQE AJSLDTQZO Q

_____

SG LDG TQZO IDGR IG DQVG Q RGI AJSLD.

_____

—SQEFD   FQSEGLLG   _____

Puzzle 2-4 *answers on page 236*

EPZ YD J TYOAPCJZ VJUH APH NMRZ

_____

LNNC ZNX VJM TRNE NM JMC DKYA NM

_____

JMC HFHOZTNCZ OXDPHD AN SHA J KYHVH?

_____

—TNTTZ   UHRANM   _____

MERRY CHRISTMAS

Puzzle 2-5 *answers on page 236*

E YQXCCZU MZDEZGELJ EL YKLQK TDKFY

_____

BWZL E BKY YEV. RXQWZI QXXN RZ QX

_____

YZZ WER EL K UZCKIQRZLQ YQXIZ KLU WZ

_____

KYNZU PXI RA KFQXJIKCW.

_____

—YWEIDZA   QZRCDZ   _____

GEBPFU NRF JMBK PK UEZ IPBFU

_____

GZKUCBV, VZU EZ JZWMKHF UM RWW

_____

GZKUCBPZF. EZ NRF JMBK R DZN,

_____

VZU EZ JZWMKHF UM RWW BRGZF.

_____

EZ NRF JMBK PK JZUEWZEZX, VZU

_____

EZ JZWMKHF UM RWW GMCKUBPZF.

_____

—HZMBHZ N. UBCZUU _____

YDBXELGHE XE NVL H LXGM NVB H

_____

EMHEVN, PIL H ELHLM VQ GXNT. LV

_____

YDMBXED SMHYM HNTWVVTJXZZ, LV PM

_____

SZMNLMVIE XN GMBYC, XE LV DHOM

_____

LDM BMHZ ESXBXL VQ YDBXELGHE.

_____

—YHZOXN YVVZXTWM _____

QXU OK AXYXYHXA ULBU ULX ZLAJKUYBK

_____

LXBAU JK B IJCJGI LXBAU, B TJFX DPXG

_____

LXBAU ULBU ULJGVK DR DULXAK RJAKU.

_____

—IXDAIX YBUULXT BFBYK

_____

LSW KUDG, UM BFC HVFY, YWIW YGMW

_____

KWV—YFVOWIECXXB YGMW KWV YSF

_____

AIFCDSL DGELM LF LSW AUAW GV LSW

_____

KUVDWI. LSWB GVNWVLWO LSW UIL

_____

FE DGNGVD JSIGMLKUM PIWMWVLM.

_____

—F. SWVIB _____

MWCHDVUTD HD VWE DETDPR NPC

_____

BHRZAHRK VWE NHCE PN WPDGHVTAHVF

_____

HR VWE WTAA, VWE KERHTA NATUE

_____

PN MWTCHVF HR VWE WETCV.

_____

—LTDWHRKVPR HCOHRK

_____

CHRISTMAS CAROLS

Puzzle 2-11 *answers on page 237*

ILFDMT MHS DRFKYAR KAD A WFQQT HAJJT DFVQ,

_____

KEMH A BFLRBFX JEJS ARZ A XVMMFR

_____

RFDS, ARZ MKF STSD YAZS FVM FI BFAQ.

_____

Puzzle 2-12 *answers on page 238*

VWKPUB QBUUO, VWKPUB QBUUO, VWKPUB TUU

HYB ETM, GY EYTH ILK WH WO HG NWSB WK T

GKB-YGNOB GCBK OUBWPY.

Puzzle 2-13 *answers on page 238*

NAFZYUX IXM NMF-PZCMF NMVPFMMN XRF

R SMNQ CXVPQ PZCM, RPF VH QZA MSMN

CRD VI, QZA DZAYF MSMP CRQ VI GYZDC.

Puzzle 2-14 *answers on page 238*

MG BLT NSRDB COF MN ZLRSDBKOD,

_____

KF BRXT HMJT EOJT BM KT:

_____

O UORBRSCET SG O UTOR BRTT.

_____

TRICK OR TREAT

'GMN KUC GTF BFRL CMGVTMKS GMDF UW

_____

KMSTG,

_____

CTFK VTXRVTLPRON LPCK PKO TFHH MGNFHW

_____

IRFPGTFN UXG

_____

VUKGPSMUK GU GTMN CURHO.

_____

—CMHHMPD NTPZFNYFPRF

_____

Puzzle 2-16 *answers on page 238*

RESL WUSBZXFQ DS WUSQDXFQ YHI ZSHW-

_____

ZFWWFDV JFYQDXFQ YHI DUXHWQ DUYD WS

_____

JBLN XH DUF HXWUD, WSSI ZSEI, IFZXAFE BQ!

_____

—YBDUSE BHTHSCH _____

HAPPY NEW YEAR

Puzzle 2-17 *answers on page 238*

GAUO YDQ NHMY XQHA SEYU YDQ MSNQEY

_____

NSLWU UP YDQ OHMY. NQY SY CU, PUA SY ZHM

_____

SLOQAPQVY, HEG YDHER CUG YDHY SY VHE CU.

_____

—WAUURM HYRSEMUE _____

Puzzle 2-18 *answers on page 238*

BUXI UCB IUY VBBRBV WIB LBA-TMZL DBUZ

_____

WIB QFWWBYW WFRB QMZ QBYWUS XIBBZ.

_____

—YFZ AUSWBZ YXMWW

_____

GIVING THANKS

Puzzle 2-19 *answers on page 239*

OQD AUSEZUIV IJYD VDTDH OUIDV IFZD

_____

EZJTDV OQJH QROV. HF JIDZUWJHV QJTD

_____

LDDH IFZD UIAFTDZUVQDY OQJH OQDVD

_____

PQF, HDTDZOQDSDVV, VDO JVUYD

_____

J YJK FC OQJHBVEUTUHE.

_____

—Q. R. PDVODZIJKDZ _____

EXSFAWZJTJFZ CSV JW S OQIQU, ER WQE

_____

JF EXQ XQSHEW RN XRFQWE PQF; GBE GQ

_____

DSHQNBU EXSE VRB CR FRE ESAQ EXQ

_____

CSV, SFC UQSTQ RBE EXQ ZHSEJEBCQ.

_____

—Q. M. MRIQUU   _____

YHVA YZNIFLPBJBIP CANIL YZNY QA IAAK

_____

YW YZNIF PWK GWH QZNY ZA ZNL KWIA

_____

GWH VL, NIK IWY YW YAEE ZBC QZNY

_____

QA ZNJA KWIA GWH ZBC.

_____

—PAWHPA H. ZAIKHBOF _____

HINTS

Puzzle 2-1: The word "age" is found in this puzzle.

Puzzle 2-2: The word "live" is found in this puzzle.

Puzzle 2-3: The word "affairs" is found in this puzzle.

Puzzle 2-4: The word "cake" is found in this puzzle.

Puzzle 2-5: The word "store" is found in this puzzle.

Puzzle 2-6: The word "born" is found in this puzzle.

Puzzle 2-7: The word "mind" is found in this puzzle.

Puzzle 2-8: The word "heart" is found in this puzzle.

Puzzle 2-9: The word "wise" is found in this puzzle.

Puzzle 2-10: The word "fire" is found in this puzzle.

Puzzle 2-11: The word "pipe" is found in this puzzle.

Puzzle 2-12: The word "what" is found in this puzzle.

Puzzle 2-13: The word "shiny" is found in this puzzle.

Puzzle 2-14: The word "love" is found in this puzzle.

Puzzle 2-15: The word "yawn" is found in this puzzle.

Puzzle 2-16: The word "bump" is found in this puzzle.

Puzzle 2-17: The word "drop" is found in this puzzle.

Puzzle 2-18: The word "cheer" is found in this puzzle.

Puzzle 2-19: The word "graves" is found in this puzzle.

Puzzle 2-20: The word "jewel" is found in this puzzle.

Puzzle 2-21: The word "true" is found in this puzzle.

CHAPTER 3

Laughing Out Loud

A good dose of humor is a great way to break up your day, and who better to deliver those punch lines than Woody Allen, Steve Martin, Lucille Ball, Bill Cosby, and George Burns? You'll find some great one-liners from their routines and television shows in this chapter, along with a few witty sayings they delivered in conversations with others.

WOODY ALLEN

Puzzle 3-1 *answers on page 239*

ADN BCF J GKIJKHK JF VDR NAKF UTLW

_____

ICLW NKKY J VDW SM WDFVTK BCTVAW JF

_____

WAK ZDIIKZ DX CF KIKBWZJB WMOKNZJWKZ?

_____

Puzzle 3-2 *answers on page 239*

V'S FDANYRQHQ JK ZHNZEH MTN MFRA AN "XRNM"

_____

ATH YRVUHODH MTHR VA'D TFOQ HRNYLT

_____

AN CVRQ KNYO MFK FONYRQ BTVRFANMR.

_____

Puzzle 3-3 *answers on page 239*

LFDHWKCPT MFKXP KW HXPFKMH BHSPG KW

_____

LZPF RLFBA VKOOKLW TLOOHFG H APHF HWT

_____

GNPWTG ZPFA OKBBOP LW LRRKMP GENNOKPG.

_____

Puzzle 3-4 *answers on page 240*

NIDC OID RPRLDSQ PREEDL, M TRCMPJDL. M

_____

OIFZXIO OIDQ SMXIO NRCO OIDMK FBPRKB

_____

URPJ RCL OID TRNC BIFT IRB UDDC FZO FH

_____

UZBMCDBB HFK RNIMED.

_____

Puzzle 3-5 *answers on page 240*

A QTP CLIBQS BUC BZ MBXXWRW ZBI MLWTCASR

BS CLW JWCTELDPAMP WFTJ; A XBBNWK ASCB

CLW PBUX BZ CLW OBD PACCASR SWFC CB JW.

LUCILLE BALL

Puzzle 3-6 *answers on page 240*

B HNYHNL LMN ZCEEBDY IG LMN ELRABI

EVELNU. B PCE KNHV CZZHNFBCLBKN IG BL

JNFCREN B MCA DI LCXNDL.

Puzzle 3-7 *answers on page 240*

T VLTRS SRAPTRK PLCV GAI BCRRAV NA TO

DAZX TDMAZVCRV VLCR SRAPTRK PLCV

GAI BCR NA. TR ECBV, VLCV'O KAAN VCOVX.

Puzzle 3-8 *answers on page 240*

JV EMF ZWHD BMUYDIJHX GMHY, WBA W

PFBE QYSBMH DM GM JD. DIY UMSY DIJHXB

EMF GM, DIY UMSY EMF NWH GM.

Puzzle 3-9 *answers on page 240*

IWU IS LZU LZAWMT A BUQHWUG LZU ZQHG OQP

OQT LZQL AL GIUTW'L KQP LI MUL GATYIDHQMUG.

Puzzle 3-10 *answers on page 240*

L XLK RWI HINNZHUEJ CYZTTZT L RIXLK'T

LCZ XLJ OZ TXLNU, OYU WZ'T KIU SZNJ ONFCWU.

Puzzle 3-11 *answers on page 240*

BXADF'R NVE? . . . VT IXDRF'T VFTDZDRT

AD XFD EVT. V'GD EDDF RX NVEDZOTDI VT PSZTR.

GEORGE BURNS

Puzzle 3-12 *answers on page 241*

B CZQX'G HOZBODO BX CSBXL. BG'W HOOX

_____

CQXO. B'M FQURBXL QX E XOF OTBG.

_____

HOWBCOW, B YEX'G CBO XQF—B'M HQQROC.

_____

Puzzle 3-13 *answers on page 241*

QMD WRSQ LWFROQYUQ QMLUN LU YIQLUN

_____

LS MRUDSQB. LH BRP IYU HYCD QMYQ,

_____

BRP'KD NRQ LQ WYGD.

_____

Puzzle 3-14 *answers on page 241*

ALL UQM QDD AYR ERLEDR CYL VILC YLC

_____

AL TNI AYSH KLNIATG QTR UNHG TNIISIZ

_____

AQWSKQUH LT KNAASIZ YQST.

_____

Puzzle 3-15 *answers on page 241*

VXSJRQFVV JMQV HQ XU PSXHAU. NTFQ

_____

H NFQR RL VKTLLA H NSV VL VXSJR XU

_____

RFSKTFJ NSV HQ XU KASVV PLJ PHIF UFSJV.

_____

Puzzle 3-16 *answers on page 241*

K DTJ'C VJHAISCTJH XBL K WFVJNAH TPAIKDTJ

_____

BKSCEIL. XBAJ K XTS T NKH CBAIA XTS SE

_____

FKCCFA EW KC.

_____

BILL COSBY

Puzzle 3-17 *answers on page 241*

USCJD AITDYW JHI GUI XDZF VHIJGSHIW GUJG

_____

JZZXM GUITH VUTZNHID GX VXCI AJVP UXCI.

_____

Puzzle 3-18 *answers on page 241*

IXE LEVH UJVMI PGQ JW GALEVIJMJWY JM

_____

IK GLKJA IXE CKWCVEIE SVKZJME GWA

_____

CTPIJLGIE IXE AEPJYXIUTPPH LGYTE.

_____

Puzzle 3-19 *answers on page 241*

C UQS'D ISQY DGW IWX DQ PBLLWPP, RBD

_____

DGW IWX DQ EACFBVW CP DVXCSH DQ

_____

ZFWAPW WMWVXRQUX.

_____

Puzzle 3-20 answers on page 242

ZFCP PNPSYBHP PZOP GWB XTCPO VWP

_____

XFOVTCP BR MPVVFHM BZQPS, F JPMFH

_____

PTDW QTY GFVW DBRRPP THQ BJFVKTSFPO.

_____

Puzzle 3-21 answers on page 242

F YJWS QJ QHE YKLE FKI'Q IEXELLFWT—

_____

KQ'L QHE LQPMKS JIEL QHFQ IEES QHE FSCKXE.

_____

Puzzle 3-22 *answers on page 242*

JBD JPLJB AQ JBHJ EHPDXJQ HPD XOJ

_____

PDHKKU AXJDPDQJDI AX YLQJASD.

_____

JBDU YLQJ RHXJ ZLADJ.

_____

STEVE MARTIN

Puzzle 3-23 *answers on page 242*

ALTWD DVS JBKDBT DBYJ FS DVS PBBJ

_____

QSNW: L NMW PBLQP DB VMCS M JLWSMWS

_____

QMFSJ MADST FS.

_____

Puzzle 3-24 *answers on page 242*

UCE, BZCMH LYHTJZ, BZHE ZXRH X

_____

GNLLHYHTB PCYG LCY HRHYEBZNTD!

_____

Puzzle 3-25 *answers on page 242*

T YDVTDQD BCGB HDP TH BCD OUHB

_____

YDGIBTZIV, JGBIXGV, GJW RCUVDHUOD

_____

BCTJL BCGB OUJDF KGJ YIF.

_____

Puzzle 3-26 *answers on page 242*

S DSMW L UVRLC USJT L TWLH VC TWY

_____

XTVEDHWYX. S TLJW CWZMX.

_____

Puzzle 3-27 *answers on page 242*

BDKCQ VJ LDI ZVMQL CR BDKCQ VQJ'L

_____

REJJO, YEL BDKCQ VJ LDI ZVMQL CR CFMIF VQ.

_____

Puzzle 3-28 *answers on page 242*

M EXMRQ M JMJ KYAEEN ZAHH, UGRCMJAYMRL

_____

M CEPYEAJ GBE ZMEX RGEXMRL OBE P

_____

OBRUX GD OHPRQ KPKAY.

_____

Puzzle 3-29 *answers on page 243*

Y KQIYQAQ QPBQGBMYPDQPB ZMP MJOYGQ

_____

BE KQ MGB, MPN ZMP KQZEDQ MGB, KTB

_____

YV HET JQB ETB BE DMLQ MGB HET'GQ MP YNYEB.

_____

HINTS

Puzzle 3-1: The word "week" is found in this puzzle.

Puzzle 3-2: The word "find" is found in this puzzle.

Puzzle 3-3: The word "office" is found in this puzzle.

Puzzle 3-4: The word "pawn" is found in this puzzle.

Puzzle 3-5: The word "soul" is found in this puzzle.

Puzzle 3-6: The word "talent" is found in this puzzle.

Puzzle 3-7: The word "taste" is found in this puzzle.

Puzzle 3-8: The word "busy" is found in this puzzle.

Puzzle 3-9: The word "hard" is found in this puzzle.

Puzzle 3-10: The word "bright" is found in this puzzle.

Puzzle 3-11: The word "interest" is found in this puzzle.

Puzzle 3-12: The word "exit" is found in this puzzle.

Puzzle 3-13: The word "fake" is found in this puzzle.

Puzzle 3-14: The word "hair" is found in this puzzle.

Puzzle 3-15: The word "class" is found in this puzzle.

Puzzle 3-16: The word "little" is found in this puzzle.

Puzzle 3-17: The word "home" is found in this puzzle.

Puzzle 3-18: The word "avoid" is found in this puzzle.

Puzzle 3-19: The word "please" is found in this puzzle.

Puzzle 3-20: The word "begin" is found in this puzzle.

Puzzle 3-21: The word "wise" is found in this puzzle.

Puzzle 3-22: The word "quiet" is found in this puzzle.

Puzzle 3-23: The word "after" is found in this puzzle.

Puzzle 3-24: The word "those" is found in this puzzle.

Puzzle 3-25: The word "money" is found in this puzzle.

Puzzle 3-26: The word "head" is found in this puzzle.

Puzzle 3-27: The word "chaos" is found in this puzzle.

Puzzle 3-28: The word "bunch" is found in this puzzle.

Puzzle 3-29: The word "aspire" is found in this puzzle.

CHAPTER 4

Get Inspired

Motivational quotations are a thought-provoking way to get fired up about your life and make some needed changes. They also work to promote positive thinking and help you achieve success in the workplace, your relationships, and your personal life. Inspirational people like Winston Churchill, Martin Luther King, Jr., Ralph Waldo Emerson, and Mahatma Gandhi have motivated people for years, and now it's your brain's turn. These puzzles are geared toward motivating you brain and, hopefully, enriching your life.

WINSTON CHURCHILL

Puzzle 4-1 *answers on page 243*

AS AL T VALSTZX SY SIO SY UYYZ SYY FTI

_____

TPXTK. SPX QPTAH YF KXLSAHO QTH YHUO

_____

WX CITLGXK YHX UAHZ TS T SAVX.

_____

Puzzle 4-2 *answers on page 243*

DL KPVL P JXQXRC BA DWPI DL CLI, DL

_____

KPVL P JXTL BA DWPI DL CXQL.

_____

Puzzle 4-3 *answers on page 243*

CG OHEKK LZQ XESK ZR XEKQGR; CG OHEKK

_____

LZQ CGEDGL ZR QSRG . . . TSBG JO QHG

_____

QZZKO ELU CG CSKK XSLSOH QHG YZP.

_____

Puzzle 4-4 *answers on page 243*

ROJ KZIU IU ROK KZH HRM. IK IU ROK

_____

HSHR KZH GHYIRRIRY OF KZH HRM. GBK IK

_____

IU, PHNZXPU, KZH HRM OF KZH GHYIRRIRY.

_____

RALPH WALDO EMERSON

Puzzle 4-5 *answers on page 243*

JBK CGYYBQ VB G RAYVYMNN QBB NBBY

_____

EMCGKNM JBK YMOMX RYBU TBU NBBY

_____

AQ UAHH EM QBB HGQM.

_____

Puzzle 4-6 *answers on page 243*

WAIO JNGP CGANBZ VP IBZ WAIO JNGP

_____

CGTMHG VP IHG PUIJJ UIOOGHP YMULIHGZ

_____

OM WAIO JNGP WNOANB VP.

_____

XIN'R JS RII RPEPX QNX BFVSQEPBM

QJIVR UIVZ QLRPINB. QDD DPYS PB QN

SGTSZPESNR. RMS EIZS SGTSZPESNRB

UIV EQWS RMS JSRRSZ.

MAHATMA GANDHI

Puzzle 4-8 *answers on page 244*

YUP QEVVPSPBKP LPYXPPB XUOY XP QD

_____

OBQ XUOY XP OSP KOHOLNP DV QDEBJ

_____

XDCNQ ZCVVEKP YD ZDNFP IDZY DV YUP

_____

XDSNQ'Z HSDLNPIZ.

_____

BL HLUGXDK XC ALB BL HLUGKB. BVK PKUXB

JXKC XA JLDXAG XA COXBK LH BVK DXDXM

TALWJKMGK BVZB BVK LAK BVZB PICB SK

JLDKM XC ALB Z HUXKAM.

Puzzle 4-10 *answers on page 244*

Z RCBX NTWRZNI NXV WT WXCDR WRX
_____

VTJSG. WJLWR CNG NTN-BZTSXNDX CJX CU
_____

TSG CU WRX RZSSU. CSS Z RCBX GTNX ZU
_____

WT WJM XOYXJZHXNWU ZN FTWR TN CU
_____

BCUW C UDCSX CU Z DTLSG.
_____

MARTIN LUTHER KING, JR.

Puzzle 4-11 *answers on page 244*

ZTT CMBUMQKK IK CMQAZMIBEK, ZSY VFQ

_____

KBTEVIBS BP BSQ CMBWTQX WMISUK EK

_____

PZAQ VB PZAQ HIVF ZSBVFQM CMBWTQX.

_____

K ZUMKUCU JRVJ XDVAFUH JAXJR VDH

XDTBDHKJKBDVM MBCU PKMM RVCU

JRU IKDVM PBAH KD AUVMKJO. JRVJ KY

PRO AKGRJ, JUFWBAVAKMO HUIUVJUH, KY

YJABDGUA JRVD UCKM JAKXFWRVDJ.

UAJ OFUIBCUJ BJCHONJ QW C BCV IH

VQU EAJNJ AJ HUCVGH IV BQBJVUH QW

RQBWQNU CVG RQVYJVIJVRJ, TOU EAJNJ

AJ HUCVGH CU UIBJH QW RACFFJVKJ

CVG RQVUNQYJNHL.

MOTHER TERESA

Puzzle 4-14 *answers on page 245*

NXNJFCIGF OIGLF BNNUB OI CN HV BTAW

_____

L ONJJHCYN JTBW; LVZHITB KIJ EJNLONJ

_____

GNXNYIDUNVOB LVG EJNLONJ PHBWNB LVG

_____

BI IV; BI OWLO AWHYGJNV WLXN XNJF

_____

YHOOYN OHUN KIJ OWNHJ DLJNVOB.

_____

PV PK YBV RBJ ICWR JM GB, ECV RBJ ICWR

_____

QBNM JM FCV PY VRM GBPYA. PV PK YBV

_____

RBJ ICWR JM APNM, ECV RBJ ICWR QBNM

_____

JM FCV PY VRM APNPYA.

_____

Puzzle 4-16 *answers on page 245*

IJ LJW WNFLZ WNAW UJKC, FL JGICG WJ

_____

SC RCLBFLC, NAH WJ SC CQWGAJGIFLAGO.

_____

XNAW XC LCCI FH WJ UJKC XFWNJBW

_____

RCWWFLR WFGCI.

_____

OTHER MOTIVATIONAL QUOTATIONS

Puzzle 4-17 *answers on page 245*

SL NJV KGTH T WJSMG PSXKSY NJV

_____

ZTN "NJV MTYYJX QTSYX," XKGY ON TUU

_____

EGTYZ QTSYX, TYD XKTX WJSMG PSUU

_____

OG ZSUGYMGD.

_____

—WSYMGYX WTY BJBK

_____

Puzzle 4-18 *answers on page 245*

SLJ LPLAK TQX MA NMTQX HLAL, YC KMO

_____

XLPLA HLQA TL QVQYX, ALTLTWLA JHYG,

_____

JHQJ YC KMO NYGH JM WL VALQJ QJ QSS,

_____

KMO TOGJ WLVYX NHLAL KMO QAL QXE

_____

NYJH NHQJ KMO QAL. HL NHM NMOSE WL

_____

VALQJ QXKNHLAL TOGJ CYAGJ WL VALQJ

_____

YX HYG MNX DHYSQELSDHYQ.

_____

—AOGGLSS H. RMXNLSS _____

Puzzle 4-19 *answers on page 246*

OIH XFLD DLKHGD RWO NWIIHII:

_____

DFH XWWYI XWOKY QH MHSR IEKHGD EP GW

_____

QESYI ILGJ HATHND DFWIH DFLD ILGJ QHID.

_____

—FHGSR MLG YRBH _____

Puzzle 4-20 *answers on page 246*

SRMR GZ U YRZY YJ PGTA JDY BSRYSRM

_____

FJDM QGZZGJT GT IGPR GZ HJQNIRYR. GP

_____

FJD'MR UIGVR, GY GZT'Y.

_____

—MGHSUMA LUHS _____

GXLJ XI JUO RGWXTJQBJ JURBAL RB JUO

_____

DXTMC UQSO NOOB QFFXGWMRLUOC NV

_____

WOXWMO DUX UQSO KOWJ XB JTVRBA

_____

DUOB JUOTO LOOGOC JX NO BX UXWO QJ QMM.

_____

—CQMO FQTBOARO _____

OY NALBGM WNNULY KHWK KHY OWM OY

_____

NYY KHATIN AN KHY OWM KHYM SYWGGM

_____

WSY VS KHY OWM KHYM NHVUGX CY. WTX

_____

VUS WKKAKUXYN WTX CYHWQAVSN ISVO

_____

VUK VP KHYNY WNNULBKAVTN.

_____

—NKYQYT RVQYM   _____

HINTS

Puzzle 4-1: The word "chain" is found in this puzzle.

Puzzle 4-2: The word "life" is found in this puzzle.

Puzzle 4-3: The word "falter" is found in this puzzle.

Puzzle 4-4: The word "end" is found in this puzzle.

Puzzle 4-5: The word "soon" is found in this puzzle.

Puzzle 4-6: The word "lies" is found in this puzzle.

Puzzle 4-7: The word "timid" is found in this puzzle.

Puzzle 4-8: The word "suffice" is found in this puzzle.

Puzzle 4-9: The word "merit" is found in this puzzle.

Puzzle 4-10: The word "teach" is found in this puzzle.

Puzzle 4-11: The word "brings" is found in this puzzle.

Puzzle 4-12: The word "final" is found in this puzzle.

Puzzle 4-13: The word "stands" is found in this puzzle.

Puzzle 4-14: The word "rush" is found in this puzzle.

Puzzle 4-15: The word "doing" is found in this puzzle.

Puzzle 4-16: The word "tired" is found in this puzzle.

Puzzle 4-17: The word "voice" is found in this puzzle.

Puzzle 4-18: The word "hear" is found in this puzzle.

Puzzle 4-19: The word "sang" is found in this puzzle.

Puzzle 4-20: The word "find" is found in this puzzle.

Puzzle 4-21: The word "hope" is found in this puzzle.

Puzzle 4-22: The word "assume" is found in this puzzle.

CHAPTER 5

Going to the Movies

Everyone loves a good movie especially if that movie provides a memorable quote to share. You'll probably see some of your favorite expressions in this chapter, and you might learn some new ones. You may even find yourself saying them to your coworkers and friends! Enjoy solving these puzzles with lines from action adventure movies, comedies, musicals, dramas, romances, and classics, as well as some personal quotations from actors and directors about being in the business.

PERSONAL QUOTATIONS

Puzzle 5-1 *answers on page 246*

QR TQDAU AKJGEJU VJE VDHVIU FEJI SDEVR.

_____

Q UWYH WYH GQTTQSKDN QN QU VRG

_____

HWVN V AEUUI NWQRZ QN QU NY PQDD V AVR.

_____

—VDTJEG WQNSWSYSP

_____

R'HG IGGY CSRERYN COL, ERUG, BGY OL

GEGHGY PGSLV. ATGY RB BZLYV, RB'EE BZLY.

LRNTB YOA R'D JZVB BLPRY' BO VQZGGWG

BTLOZNT S HGLP BRNTB CRYSYMRSE

XGLROK, NGB BTG DOHRG OZB, SYK

XZB DP BTRYNV RY OLKGL.

—CLSYMRV COLK MOXXOES

YB WGNUO YHM SCVV URWKRSRJNKJM

_____

BS VRSM RU YHM NJYBG'U FCYX, YB

_____

RKYMGOGMY RY RU HRU OGBAVMQ, NKF

_____

YB MZOGMUU RY HRU FMFRJNYRBK.

_____

—QNGVBK AGNKFB _____

Puzzle 5-4 *answers on page 247*

HI YBXHM WUV FCV VLDUVMMBRS RY

_____

HRHVSFWUI EVMBUVM. B YRXXRT HI

_____

BSMFBSAFM, OPF BS W EBMABDXBSVE TWI.

_____

—URHWS DRXWSMJB _____

Puzzle 5-5 *answers on page 247*

PY LXGRASR SOAL RB PX RVX BRVXT LOY,

_____

A'IX XGBMQV NTBFCXPS AG PY CAHX, SB

_____

UVY SVBMCL A SXX YBMT HACPS?

_____

—LOIAL ZTBGXGFXTQ _____

ACTION/ADVENTURE MOVIES

Puzzle 5-6 *answers on page 247*

Lawrence of Arabia

R JRF SVD TMGGI GOMI, GOLM JM, JMNMGY

_____

VOAMI TVM TNCTV. BCT R JRF SVD TMGGI

_____

VRGQ-GOMI VRI QDNKDTTMF SVMNM VM HCT OT.

_____

—ZGRCAM NROFI _____

Ben-Hur

ORY PWI DEKWG W UWI'L LGYJJ. ORY PWI

_____

WEEKLF QAU. ORY PWI FQERH QAU AIFR

_____

W MYIVKRI. DYF QRH MR ORY CAVQF WI AMKW?

_____

—WIMEK UREKJJ _____

Puzzle 5-8 *answers on page 248*
Platoon

Y ZFYER ELW, KLLRYEQ BTHR, WD SYS ELZ

_____

XYQFZ ZFD DEDMJ, WD XLPQFZ LPVCDKADC.

_____

ZFD DEDMJ WTC YE PC. ZFD WTV YC

_____

LADV XLV MD ELW, BPZ YZ WYKK TKWTJC

_____

BD ZFDVD, ZFD VDCZ LX MJ STJC.

_____

—HFTVKYD CFDDE _____

Puzzle 5-9 *answers on page 248*
Jurassic Park

DQFS, VZW DGZM TNCQRWCTWT JQMQ TG

_____

LMQGNNZLCQI JCWS JSQWSQM GM RGW

_____

WSQD NGZHI, WSQD ICIR'W TWGL WG

_____

WSCRK CX WSQD TSGZHI.

_____

—YQXX EGHIVHZP _____

Braveheart

X QXNN MYNN HLU LK QXNNXBG QBNNBVY.

_____

CXWMLEXBOW QXNN VBNN GY B NXBE,

_____

ZUM CXWMLEH XW QEXMMYO ZH MCLWY

_____

QCL'JY CBOSYA CYELYW.

_____

—BOSUW GBVKBHAYO _____

ANIMATED MOVIES

Puzzle 5-11 *answers on page 248*
Aladdin

RA WM FP AOQ FNURMZ, UEYV N RVDQI

_____

OAETS WM IZMNRMZ RVNQ NTT RVM

_____

RZMNUEZM NQS NTT RVM FNIDY DQ RVM OAZTS.

_____

—ZAWDQ ODTTDNFU _____

Puzzle 5-12 *answers on page 248*
Mulan

YEG XOKQGB YEPY VOKKTA RM PDFGBARYI

_____

RA YEG BPBGAY PMD TKAY VGPZYRXZO KX POO.

_____

—NPY TKBRYPV _____

Puzzle 5-13 *answers on page 248*
Alice in Wonderland

GITH SNSPKIYS'T GVC USPS. KIB GVK UVNS

_____

YIHJRSC HUVH J'G YIH VEE HUSPS GKTSEX.

_____

—THSPEJYD UIEEIOVK _____

Puzzle 5-14 *answers on page 248*
Toy Story

O'P VSUP PCWWML. TMLL, CZWICLLG O'P VSUP

_____

C EPCLLMS ZUPNCHG WJCW TCE NISZJCEMQ

_____

AG PCWWML OH C LMRMSCXMQ AIGUIW.

_____

—TCLLCZM EJCTH _____

Puzzle 5-15 *answers on page 249*
The Lion King

XWOFG, CBN OB NBCC SPY XPOBNZWEM

_____

OS HGNZBI NPCD OB. CPPJ GN NZB XNGIX,

_____

NZB MIBGN JWEMX PH NZB TGXN GIB YT

_____

NZBIB, UGNLZWEM PABI YX.

_____

—QGOBX BGIC QPEBX _____

CHAPTER 5: GOING TO THE MOVIES

CLASSIC MOVIES

Puzzle 5-16 *answers on page 249*
Gone with the Wind

I FHV'E EKIVQ HTGDE EKHE YIXKE VGJ. IR I OG,

_____

I'WW XG FYHLU. I'WW EKIVQ HTGDE EKHE

_____

EGNGYYGJ.

_____

—BIBIMV WMIXK _____

Puzzle 5-17 *answers on page 249*
It Happened One Night

N EILQNK SDQNE WYJER ZIDKFE'X KJCY DEFYL XSY

_____

UNQY LIIO HJXS SYL HJXSIDX RIJER EDXXB!

_____

—ZKNLG RNWKY _____

It's a Wonderful Life

EPA DUU, YUPMYU, EPA'ZU MUQJJE NQV Q

_____

XPWVUMTAJ JCTU. VPW'R EPA DUU XNQR Q

_____

SCDRQHU CR XPAJV OU RP LADR

_____

RNMPX CR QXQE?

_____

—NUWME RMQZUMD _____

Puzzle 5-19 *answers on page 249*
Mr. Smith Goes to Washington

HPI QZZ, KPHQ DPWCZR AVJR RVZOW

_____

EPIMRWH SZJMQ KH YIQR WZJLOMC RVZ

_____

NJML PD RVZ DWZZ OM VOQRPWH KPPFQ.

_____

—YJSZQ QRZAJWR _____

Puzzle 5-20 *answers on page 249*
Breakfast at Tiffany's

G'UD EQY YQ MQ BQXDYNGOE KCQHY YND

_____

FKR G AQQI. G XDKO, K EGTA WHBY PKO'Y

_____

EQ YQ BGOE BGOE FGYN K ETDDO ZKPD.

_____

—KHMTDR NDJCHTO _____

COMEDIES

Puzzle 5-21 *answers on page 250*
Forrest Gump

POXQ OI POBQ Y ECT CX VWCVCPYJQI. SCU

_____

FQAQR BFCM MWYJ SCU'RQ LCOFL JC LQJ.

_____

—JCG WYFBI _____

Puzzle 5-22 *answers on page 250*
The Truman Show

GKKS QKMHDHG! BHS DH OBJW D SKH'R JWW

_____

PKA: GKKS BNRWMHKKH, GKKS WYWHDHG,

_____

BHS GKKS HDGER!

_____

—IDQ OBMMWP _____

KMQ FQN LMIFQ VIIU'T MQYQ! KMQ FQN

_____

LMIFQ VIIU'T MQYQ! KMHT HT KMQ UHFS IW

_____

TLIFKBFQIGT LGVZHDHKX H FQQS! CX FBCQ

_____

HF LYHFK! KMBK YQBZZX CBUQT TICQVISX!

_____

KMHFJT BYQ JIHFJ KI TKBYK MBLLQFHFJ

_____

KI CQ FIN.

_____

—TKQAQ CBYKHF   _____

Puzzle 5-24 *answers on page 250*
Patch Adams

VYF WOLKW K ZQTLKTL—VYF NQB, VYF

_____

PYTL. SFW Q XFKOKBWLL, VYF WOLKW K

_____

RLOTYB KBZ VYF NQB BY EKWWLO WAL YFWMYEL.

_____

—OYSQB NQPPQKET _____

Puzzle 5-25 *answers on page 250*
Airplane

XEMDRX, FHA'OX M BXBJXO HK SPDL VOXZ.

_____

VMR FHA KMVX LHBX ARGEXMLMRS KMVSL?

_____

—EXLEDX RDXELXR _____

Puzzle 5-26 *answers on page 250*
Happy Gilmore

O UPC'L EWBOWRW JAH'NW P SNAYWVVOACPB

_____

XABYWN. O LFOCM JAH VFAHBZ EW DANMOCX

_____

PL LFW VCPUM EPN.

_____

—EAE EPNMWN _____

DRAMATIC/ROMANTIC MOVIES

Puzzle 5-27 *answers on page 251*

Sleepless in Seattle

JYAKNMU NA AIFYKCNMH PY'OY NMOYMKYJ

_____

GYXSQAY PY XSM'K AKSMJ KCY WSXK KCSK

_____

YOYTUKCNMH KCSK CSVVYMA NA SXXNJYMKSB.

_____

—FYH TUSM _____

Puzzle 5-28 *answers on page 251*
Beaches

LPT'KD UPNNZ FRW Z YRNNYD, YPGD Z YRNNYD,

_____

ZWJ ZYFZLG AZKD NAD IYTDG BTGN Z YRNNYD;

_____

NAZN'G NAD GNPQL PE, NAD UYPQL PE YPKD.

_____

—IDNND XRJYDQ _____

Puzzle 5-29 *answers on page 251*
Steel Magnolias

R HLEFG TQYWAT WQXA YWRTYJ KRBEYAU

_____

LD HLBGATDEF YWQB Q FRDAYRKA LD

_____

BLYWRBZ UPANRQF.

_____

—MEFRQ TLSATYU _____

Puzzle 5-30 *answers on page 251*
Hope Floats

XGSXRG KVRR CN RSFG. TUGI KVRR ZCJUT

_____

HVEO SWT. CT UVXXGNQ VRR TUG TCBG.

_____

—QVNLZV HWRRSEO _____

Puzzle 5-31 *answers on page 251*
When Harry Met Sally

D HKGS BSCS LPTDWBL MSHKIYS FBST OPI

_____

CSKVDZS OPI FKTL LP YJSTR LBS CSYL PU

_____

OPIC VDUS FDLB YPGSMPRO, OPI FKTL LBS

_____

CSYL PU OPIC VDUS LP YLKCL KY

_____

YPPT KY JPYYDMVS.

_____

—MDVVO HCOYLKV _____

City of Angels

R XKCFM SYWOQS OYUQ OYM KDQ JSQYWO

_____

KP OQS OYRS, KDQ BRHH PSKL OQS

_____

LKCWO, KDQ WKCZO KP OQS OYDM, WOYD

_____

QWQSDRWA XRWOKCW RW.

_____

—DRZKFYH ZYEQ _____

MUSICALS

Puzzle 5-33 *answers on page 252*
West Side Story

ZIKB GD GHX AIYUR GYB AIYU. ZIKB GD

_____

GHX ABIXMR GYB ABIXM. ZIKB GD GHX

_____

VGOR GYB NIRM VGO. GYNF UBIMA OJNN

_____

EIXM HR YGO.

_____

—XJLAIXU WBFZBX   _____

AE RJRVH TGQ UOIU PMBU QR XGER, UORVR

_____

AB IE RWRPREU GD DME. HGM DAEX UOR

_____

DME IEX—BEIF—UOR TGQ'B I KIPR.

_____

—TMWAR IEXVRSB _____

Willy Wonka and the Chocolate Factory

EN PRO IBDG GR VEYI SBXBAEMY, MEKSFP

_____

FRRW BXRODA BDA VEYI EG. BDPGLEDZ

_____

PRO IBDG GR, AR EG. IBDG GR CLBDZY

_____

GLY IRXFA? GLYXY'M DRGLEDZ GR EG.

_____

—ZYDY IEFAYX   _____

EARDN DKU DNUFVD HM OLIVAYANM. NKUC

_____

DKU DNUFVD HM VFBMUR, HM NRAFV PFNU.

_____

FCP CZB DKU DNUFVD HM XZPPFHC XFRNUR.

_____

—YFNKURACU WUNF-GZCUD

_____

All That Jazz

LC L HLD, L'K YMVVN CMV WAA SOD QWH

_____

SOLEUY L HLH SM NMZ. WEH LC L ALPD,

_____

L'K YMVVN CMV WAA SOD QWH SOLEUY

_____

L'K UMEEW HM SM NMZ.

_____

—VMN YRODLHDV _____

Puzzle 5-38 *answers on page 252*
Singin' in the Rain

ZT WB OKZDL G XZSSXB IRN ZDSR NRFK

_____

JFPEKFP XZYBM, ZS PGCBM FM TBBX GM

_____

ZT RFK JGKE WRKC GZD'S OBBD ZD YGZD

_____

TRK DRSJZDL.

_____

—IBGD JGLBD _____

ZKFHF XWC JMNF WJJ WHMLUT, ILZ E UFNFH

_____

KFWHT EZ CEUQEUQ. UM E UFNFH KFWHT

_____

EZ WZ WJJ, ZEJJ ZKFHF XWC SML.

_____

—CKEHJFS PMUFC _____

HINTS

Puzzle 5-1: The word "messy" is found in this puzzle.

Puzzle 5-2: The word "squeeze" is found in this puzzle.

Puzzle 5-3: The word "duty" is found in this puzzle.

Puzzle 5-4: The word "films" is found in this puzzle.

Puzzle 5-5: The word "life" is found in this puzzle.

Puzzle 5-6: The word "truth" is found in this puzzle.

Puzzle 5-7: The word "skull" is found in this puzzle.

Puzzle 5-8: The word "enemy" is found in this puzzle.

Puzzle 5-9: The word "scientists" is found in this puzzle.

Puzzle 5-10: The word "liar" is found in this puzzle

Puzzle 5-11: The word "magic" is found in this puzzle.

Puzzle 5-12: The word "blooms" is found in this puzzle.

Puzzle 5-13: The word "mad" is found in this puzzle.

Puzzle 5-14: The word "company" is found in this puzzle.

Puzzle 5-15: The word "stars" is found in this puzzle.

Puzzle 5-16: The word "crazy" is found in this puzzle.

Puzzle 5-17: The word "human" is found in this puzzle.

Puzzle 5-18: The word "life" is found in this puzzle.

Puzzle 5-19: The word "forget" is found in this puzzle.

Puzzle 5-20: The word "face" is found in this puzzle.

Puzzle 5-21: The word "box" is found in this puzzle.

Puzzle 5-22: The word "night" is found in this puzzle.

Puzzle 5-23: The word "print" is found in this puzzle.

Puzzle 5-24: The word "person" is found in this puzzle.

Puzzle 5-25: The word "crew" is found in this puzzle.

Puzzle 5-26: The word "snack" is found in this puzzle.

Puzzle 5-27: The word "destiny" is found in this puzzle.

Puzzle 5-28: The word "glory" is found in this puzzle.

Puzzle 5-29: The word "thirty" is found in this puzzle.

Puzzle 5-30: The word "fall" is found in this puzzle.

Puzzle 5-31: The word "soon" is found in this puzzle.

Puzzle 5-32: The word "hair" is found in this puzzle.

Puzzle 5-33: The word "vow" is found in this puzzle.

Puzzle 5-34: The word "game" is found in this puzzle.

Puzzle 5-35: The word "world" is found in this puzzle.

Puzzle 5-36: The word "trial" is found in this puzzle.

Puzzle 5-37: The word "live" is found in this puzzle.

Puzzle 5-38: The word "vain" is found in this puzzle.

Puzzle 5-39: The word "love" is found in this puzzle.

CHAPTER 6

It's All Politics

People have been practicing the art of politics through the ages, and we're not the only ones. We can observe politics in the form of dominant hierarchies or pecking orders in various animal species. The puzzles you'll be solving in this chapter are related to politics and include quotations from famous kings and queens, prime ministers, U.S. presidents and vice presidents, and other world leaders. Some of the quotations are political in nature, some offer advice on ruling and leadership, and some are just humorous and silly.

KINGS AND QUEENS

Puzzle 6-1 *answers on page 253*

T VTN GHZII Z FTOYUTQ TB SZOYV NUII VTIK

_____

PG NVSQ NS ZOS KSZK, NVT ZHMUYUTPGID GSSW

_____

ZBYSO YVS NVTIS NTOIK NVUIS NS ZOS IUXUQJ.

_____

—FVUIUF UU _____

Puzzle 6-2 *answers on page 253*

EX JXBS DSRBW EXV; L VLFF DZLEQ

_____

HPXE BSOSENS.

_____

—JRBM IHSSE XT WCXDW _____

Puzzle 6-3 *answers on page 253*

HFF ECXHDZS HDR CSXXJKFS SUSDCE HXS

_____

BSFQOPS, KVC QOPWOXCE BS RSEAJES.

_____

—QFSOAHCXH   _____

Puzzle 6-4 *answers on page 253*

DZ DI ACNCIIJWL ZS ZWL ZS IFWHJII SACICGP

_____

JGUJLI; ZTDI SNNFHJZDSA SFBTZ ZS GJIZ

_____

JI GSAB JI GDPC.

_____

—QFCCA NTWDIZDAJ   _____

Puzzle 6-5 *answers on page 253*

R HEJK OSQWX RC RZNSYYRBLK CS AEDDT

_____

CHK HKEJT BQDXKW SO DKYNSWYRBRLRCT . . .

_____

—GRWP KXUEDX JRRR _____

Puzzle 6-6 *answers on page 253*

LBY GBSCY GSWCX IR IK WYVSCL. RSSK

_____

LBYWY GICC ZY SKCA EIVY DIKMR CYEL—LBY

_____

DIKM SE YKMCPKX, LBY DIKM SE RQPXYR,

_____

LBY DIKM SE NCFZR, LBY DIKM SE BYPWLR,

_____

PKX LBY DIKM SE XIPUSKXR.

_____

—DIKM EPWSFD _____

PRIME MINISTERS

Puzzle 6-7 *answers on page 254*

YMGWAEIZLA JIZLWJN GKNZ ZED ZW ULJY

_____

QIDN ZW NZIESM ZCM ZMEEWELNZ IJY ZCM

_____

CLPIABME WU ZCM WXDVMJ WU FKOHLALZD

_____

WJ QCLAC ZCMD YMFMJY.

_____

—GIEVIEMZ ZCIZACME _____

OUBJS BAWZUCW OSAEXAOKJ AH MVSSJE,

_____

MCW OSAEXAOKJ BAWZUCW OUBJS AH

_____

RCWAKJ. WZAH AH V OVSWN UR

_____

YUGJSEPJEW, VEL A BAKK KJVL AW VH V

_____

OVSWN UR YUGJSEPJEW.

_____

—WUEN MKVAS _____

HJMWM IV UNM EUPPUN BFEHUW HJFH

_____

VJUOGC AM MVVMNHIFG HU RJFHMZMW

_____

SFWGIFPMNHFWT WMBUWPV FWM

_____

VOLLMVHMC . . . HJM NMMC BUW LWMFHMW

_____

WMEULNIHIUN UB HJM EWOEIFG WUGM UB

_____

HJM INCIZICOFG PMPAMW UB SFWGIFPMNH.

_____

—SFOG PFWHIN _____

R SCZ'L LNRZF LNBDB'Q KZX DBKQCZ CZ

_____

BKDLN YNX GBCGMB QNCIMS NKWB KUUBQQ

_____

LC KILCOKLRU KZS QBORKILCOKLRU

_____

YBKGCZQ IZMBQQ LNBX'DB RZ LNB

_____

ORMRLKDX CD RZ LNB GCMRUB.

_____

—PCNZ NCYKDS _____

VC SDUC MZJ CJCNMDY DYYHCT DMK

_____

VC SDUC MZJ ECNECJIDY CMCRHCT. ZIN

_____

HMJCNCTJT DNC CJCNMDY DMK ECNECJIDY

_____

DMK JSZTC HMJCNCTJT HJ HT ZIN KIJB JZ PZYYZV.

_____

—YZNK EDYRCNTJZM _____

U.S. PRESIDENTS

Puzzle 6-12 *answers on page 255*

D GVXVWZ DWG HDWTL VIDHYWDZYKW KM

_____

ZQV DXZS KM OKFVCWHVWZ SQKNTG WKZ

_____

KWTL EV ZKTVCDZVG, ENZ VWXKNCDOVG.

_____

—PYTTYDH QDCCYSKW _____

JOG BIDHVX IS JOG AEGMHVAU RIYGMUEGUJ

_____

HN JI DGAYG JOGHM VHJHZGUN SMGG,

_____

UGHJOGM MGNJMAHUHUR UIM AHFHUR

_____

JOGE HU JOGHM BWMNWHJN.

_____

—JOIEAN CGSSGMNIU _____

VRECMADCAL SY ARL MCJYRA; SL SY ARL

_____

CKRHPCAL; SL SY NRMGC. KSBC NSMC, SL

_____

SY J QJAVCMRPY YCMEJAL JAQ J

_____

NCJMNPK DJYLCM.

_____

—VCRMVC ZJYOSAVLRA _____

TQL RD, VP CUWWDH TVUMGNTQR: TRS

_____

QDX HFTX PDZM NDZQXMP NTQ LD CDM

_____

PDZ—TRS HFTX PDZ NTQ LD CDM

_____

PDZM NDZQXMP.

_____

—EDFQ C. SUQQULP _____

ESRZTAHZAB HDUB XZZY YVFZ PJBC BCZ

_____

FCVAEJAE AZZQU SW SDT UBVBZ VAQ JBU

_____

YZSYOZ BS KZ UDTZ BCVB ESRZTAHZAB FVA

_____

WDOWJOO JBU OZEJBJHVBZ SKOJEVBJSAU.

_____

—TSAVOQ TZVEVA _____

PRESIDENTIAL JOKES

Puzzle 6-17 *answers on page 255*

US'AS KMM PKVKCMS FO GBZEKHSZ, CJE

_____

B IF NFE PKAS EF SNMBYWESN QFJ FN

_____

EWS GBZEKHSZ US GKQ FA GKQ NFE WKXS GKIS.

_____

—YSFAYS U. CJZW _____

Puzzle 6-18 *answers on page 256*

BCZR DCZ QLZJKOZRD ONZJ KD, DCFD UZFRJ

_____

DCFD KD'J RND KMMZEFM.

_____

—LKACFLO RKINR _____

XIUDNDZC DC AIN R ORW XQIHKCCDIA. DH

_____

BIG CGZZKKW NYKQK RQK TRAB QKFRQWC,

_____

DH BIG WDCLQRZK BIGQCKUH BIG ZRA

_____

RUFRBC FQDNK R OIIS.

_____

—QIARUW QKRLRA _____

Puzzle 6-20 *answers on page 256*

P UPMO CVO JTG. CVAC'W NVAC P'UU RPWW

_____

CVO RTWC . . . P'R QTC WEZO AQLGTBL

_____

OXOZ UPMOB CVPW AW REIV AW P'XO UPMOB PC.

_____

—GPUU IUPQCTQ _____

Puzzle 6-21 *answers on page 256*

YS DGVS G OWNP LJPPWZPSXZ ZJ XGZJ, YS GNS

_____

G UGNZ JO XGZJ. YS DGVS G OWNP LJPPWZPSXZ

_____

ZJ SENJUS, YS GNS G UGNZ JO SENJUS.

_____

—FSJNFS Y. IEBD _____

U.S. VICE PRESIDENTS

Puzzle 6-22 *answers on page 256*

PE TFQQGN REB RFNA QRG ZEVV, AGOGFQ

_____

TJMRQ VGNIG FV BGZZ FV IJXQENL QE

_____

VRFUG QRG VEKZ FPA ZGQ QRG MZENL EKQ.

_____

—FZ MENG _____

Puzzle 6-23 *answers on page 256*

A FCJV NCTV BMMT UPTBNVQKE AQ KFV ICEK. A

_____

FCJV NCTV BMMT UPTBNVQKE AQ KFV ZPKPOV.

_____

—TCQ DPCYGV _____

SKE IZF SRELI IRHF RN IZF ZRLIKEM KS

_____

HONJRNX, KNF GFNFEOIRKN YRIFEOYYM

_____

ZOL IZF PKAFE IK XFLIEKM IZF POLI, IZF

_____

PEFLFNI, ONX IZF STITEF, IZF PKAFE IK

_____

DERNG IRHF IK ON FNX.

_____

—ZTDFEI Z. ZTHPZEFM

_____

ZVGOIVGKAC LFKT KTA ZTVFZA, KTA BYAIFZBG

_____

XAVXMA LVDMC ZTVVWA KTA XVMFZAYBG'W

_____

KIDGZTAVG VJAI KTA BGBIZTFWK'W RVYR.

_____

—WXFIV K. BUGAL _____

OD OQ CQQCGDOJR DKJD AC CGJTRC

YINGB ZCIZRC DI QCC DKCEQCRHCQ

JQ ZJUDOPOZJGDQ OG IGC IL DKC EIQD

CFPODOGB CUJQ OG KOQDIUY, JGM DI KJHC

J QCGQC IL ZNUZIQC OG UCRJDOIG DI OD.

—GCRQIG UIPVCLCRRCU

WORLD LEADERS

RQXCI CHX WCH EPHX TPAXHWYD NZCU

_____

SYUI. AX QPU'N CDDPA PYH XUXERXI NP

_____

ZCBX SYUI, AZJ IZPYDQ AX CDDPA NZXE

_____

NP ZCBX RQXCI?

_____

—VPIXW INCDRU _____

Y XSKZW BOARUB UVPUZ SARUBF YQ

_____

ARU NQSXZUWTU SI XROA YF UVPUZZUQA

_____

AROQ YQ ARU UVAUQA SI GJ LSXUBF

_____

OQW WSGYQYSQ.

_____

—OZUVOQWUB ARU TBUOA

_____

Puzzle 6-29 *answers on page 257*

K YHNHU SKS MYIGZKYE MCXYH. OZMGHNHU

_____

OMJ MFFXWBCKJZHS KY GZKJ FXPYGUI OMJ

_____

MFFXWBCKJZHS FXCCHFGKNHCI.

_____

—EXCSM WHKU _____

Puzzle 6-30 *answers on page 257*

QGFAF FSPHQH KO UOEPQPMPDK PK PKCPD

_____

CDAPKX FKOZXG QO DQQFNUQ QO FSUEDPK

_____

QO QGF NDHHFH QGDQ MOLH MDK IF FDQFK.

_____

—PKCPAD XDKCGP _____

HINTS

Puzzle 6-1: The word "portion" is found in this puzzle.

Puzzle 6-2: The word "tears" is found in this puzzle.

Puzzle 6-3: The word "events" is found in this puzzle.

Puzzle 6-4: The word "life" is found in this puzzle.

Puzzle 6-5: The word "heavy" is found in this puzzle.

Puzzle 6-6: The word "revolt" is found in this puzzle.

Puzzle 6-7: The word "starve" is found in this puzzle.

Puzzle 6-8: The word "party" is found in this puzzle.

Puzzle 6-9: The word "role" is found in this puzzle.

Puzzle 6-10: The word "access" is found in this puzzle.

Puzzle 6-11: The word "allies" is found in this puzzle.

Puzzle 6-12: The word "manly" is found in this puzzle.

Puzzle 6-13: The word "free" is found in this puzzle.

Puzzle 6-14: The word "force" is found in this puzzle.

Puzzle 6-15: The word "ask" is found in this puzzle.

Puzzle 6-16: The word "pace" is found in this puzzle.

Puzzle 6-17: The word "care" is found in this puzzle.

Puzzle 6-18: The word "does" is found in this puzzle.

Puzzle 6-19: The word "book" is found in this puzzle.

Puzzle 6-20: The word "job" is found in this puzzle.

Puzzle 6-21: The word "firm" is found in this puzzle.

Puzzle 6-22: The word "loss" is found in this puzzle.

Puzzle 6-23: The word "good" is found in this puzzle.

Puzzle 6-24: The word "time" is found in this puzzle.

Puzzle 6-25: The word "over" is found in this puzzle.

Puzzle 6-26: The word "young" is found in this puzzle.

Puzzle 6-27: The word "guns" is found in this puzzle.

Puzzle 6-28: The word "excel" is found in this puzzle.

Puzzle 6-29: The word "alone" is found in this puzzle.

Puzzle 6-30: The word "daring" is found in this puzzle.

CHAPTER 7

Religion and Spirituality

Religion accommodates all styles of worship; it may be shared by a large community or may be very personal. There are many interpretations of what constitutes religion, but it typically includes an object of devotion and a method of proper behavior, in regard to how you live your life and relate to the world around you, meant to glorify that object. The cryptograms you'll be solving in this chapter include quotations related to Christianity, Judaism, Buddhism, Confucianism, and Native American spirituality; there are also general quotations about religion and God.

ABOUT RELIGIOUS BELIEF

Puzzle 7-1 *answers on page 258*

E MVQQIT MIQMNEFN IA V SIX BLI RNBVRXH

_____

VQX CUQEHLNH LEH MRNVTURNH, IR LVH

_____

V BEZZ IA TLN TPCN IA BLEML BN VRN

_____

MIQHMEIUH EQ IURHNZFNH.

_____

—VZDNRT NEQHTNEQ _____

Puzzle 7-2 *answers on page 258*

OI MLLGFI DLFM CLFNLK NE JDYJ NK Y UXM

_____

YWIJDNWU FNPL JDL JTYMNJNXWYF EXTJ

_____

LRNEJE, XAT BATNXENJI YWM NWJLFFNULWBL

_____

YTL GTXVNMLM CI EABD Y UXM. SL SXAFM

_____

CL AWYGGTLBNYJNVL XK JDXEL UNKJE . . .

_____

NK SL EAGGTLEELM XAT GYEENXW JX

_____

LRGFXTL JDL AWNVLTEL YWM XATELFVLE.

_____

—BYTF EYUYW _____

ZIFG NVANSV RVFEMFVSG UA FAC DMKW CA

_____

JV KIMFCK, IFU MC MK NAKKMJSV CWIC KAZV

_____

DWA ITWMVQV AP IKNMPV CA KIMFCWAAU

_____

WIQV FVQVP WIU ZETW CVZNCICMAF CA JV

_____

WEZIF JVMFRK.

_____

—RVAPRV APDVSS _____

UJW SN YVRIIM JFIM RFJZQVY RYZSNZ. QV

_____

SFGVFZVW ZQV USYRAAV, ZQV VIVXQRFZ,

_____

RFW ZQV ORZ. QV QRN FJ YVRI NZMIV. QV

_____

HPNZ CVVXN JF ZYMSFU JZQVY ZQSFUN.

_____

—XRTIJ XSORNNJ _____

YEXYTE DRJIMXW VIEMF CXG RDVEF VIEMF

_____

XKW OWGEFJVRWGMWC. VIEB ARZE VIEMF

_____

CXG DMFJV RWG KXFJIMY IMA RDVEFKRFGJ.

_____

—XJNRF KMTGE _____

Puzzle 7-6 *answers on page 259*

SY AIRC I WYVOSORC PCEOQOYT OV TYS

TCKCVVIPM. SY GC OT AIPHYTM FOSA

MYZPVCEX ITB SAC ZTORCPVC OV FAIS

KYZTSV, ITB SAOV OV WYVVOGEC FOSAYZS

WYVOSORC ITB VWCKOXOK XYPHZEISOYT

OT FYPBV.

—LYAITT FYEXQITQ RYT QYCSAC

TEACHINGS OF BUDDHA

Puzzle 7-7 *answers on page 259*

CP BENC UDCU BV ENONAGFNE CPE FRU

_____

BPUG CYUBGP BV JGMN BJFGMUCPU UDCP

_____

CP BENC UDCU NSBVUV GPAT CV CP BENC.

_____

Puzzle 7-8 *answers on page 259*

RN HND NKVMMADV JBAD TNF BAKV MVZVYKVR,

_____

HNM VHKT NDBVMP. BV JBN VHKYVP NDBVMP

_____

RNVP HND NODAYH QVAZV NX WYHR.

_____

Puzzle 7-9 *answers on page 259*

MR JG XAWG XU Q UDRFM FRQA MR

AGQMD QZA MR JG AXWXIGZM XU Q OQC

RE WXEG; ERRWXUD LGRLWG QFG XAWG,

OXUG LGRLWG QFG AXWXIGZM.

Puzzle 7-10 *answers on page 259*

FCMBU GZPV LGV DCFVM LC ECLG BVULMCR

ZJB GVZX. FGVJ FCMBU ZMV ECLG LMNV

ZJB IKJB, LGVR YZJ YGZJSV CNM FCMXB.

QZ JOG DXNB BKUM Q DXOB UWOGM MKN

ROBNP OZ VQFQXV, JOG BOGEH XOM ENM

U TQXVEN ANUE RUTT BQMKOGM TKUPQXV

QM QX TOAN BUJ.

ANM GVECYNAH LN VBND JDK AOHN WOAA

LN NJYONC. J YBVVD VH YJAM OD J FAJYY VH

WJMNC TJUNY MRN WJMNC EDKCODUJLAN.

J YBVVD VH YJAM OD J AJUN OY

JATVYM EDDVMOXNK.

PXRSEUI XU LX MUIVC EJ REBV ICMJQEUI M

_____

PXL NXMR GELP LPV EULVUL XA LPCXGEUI

_____

EL ML JXTVXUV VRJV; KXW MCV LPV XUV

_____

GPX IVLJ FWCUVS.

_____

CONFUCIAN THOUGHT

Puzzle 7-14 *answers on page 260*

ORS DJT CU ZKQONS DJMSW ORS

_____

BKUUKGNLOF OC VS CZSQGCDS RKW

_____

UKQWO VNWKTSWW, JTB WNGGSWW CTLF

_____

J WNVWSANSTO GCTWKBSQJOKCT.

_____

Puzzle 7-15 *answers on page 260*

Q LKWI EJD NIIE K YIHNJE ALJ FJWIV

_____

WQHDBI, JH JEI ALJ LKDIV ALKD AKN EJD

_____

WQHDBJBN. LI ALJ FJWIV WQHDBI AJBFV

_____

INDIIX EJDLQEG KCJWI QD.

_____

Puzzle 7-16 *answers on page 260*

GZF RFTQDTKD RBGFA IGLKOKDK LGD OL

_____

LTVTF XQBBOLR, JZD OL FOKOLR TVTFA

_____

DOHT ET XQBB.

_____

Puzzle 7-17 *answers on page 260*

WPQR OEB CE MER WQMR CEMD RE

_____

OEBXUDHF, CE MER CE RE ERPDXU.

_____

Puzzle 7-18 *answers on page 260*

CFZU CZ JZZ EZU WT CWMDF, CZ JFWLXK

_____

DFSUP WT ZGLRXSUI DFZE; CFZU CZ JZZ EZU WT

_____

R AWUDMRMQ AFRMRADZM, CZ JFWLXK DLMU

_____

SUCRMKJ RUK ZYRESUZ WLMJZXBZJ.

_____

NATIVE AMERICAN FAITHS

Puzzle 7-19 *answers on page 261*

JUIMDB MS NJJ MWD MDNOWDCI UB MWD

_____

PSSTI. PNMOW MWD MCDDI, MWD NBUGNJI

_____

NBT NJJ MWD JUVUBY MWUBYI—ASR'JJ

_____

JDNCB GSCD XCSG MWDG MWNB HSSQI.

_____

—FSD OSAWUI _____

B PNQV FQNBI PEREXH ER HNNONO BHO

_____

ITN YBH JTX TBR EI YURI AXWWXJ EI BR

_____

ITN NBFWN RNNCR ITN ONNDNRI GWUN

_____

XA ITN RCV.

_____

—ZQBKV TXQRN

YHK BEKLY NMFEFY THFKG UHX EJOKN

_____

LIXRK LOO UFOO NWFOK JMXZ YHFN OLZP

_____

. . . LZP YHFN YFWK YHK FZPFLZ ELTK FN

_____

ULFYFZB LZP MELAFZB.

_____

—THFKG DXNKMH _____

Puzzle 7-22 *answers on page 261*

RZZ PVTIN NPRHY JPY NRMY CHYRJP—

_____

JPY CYRNJ, JPY JHYY, JPY MRT, JPY RVH

_____

NPRHYN VJN NFVHVJ KVJP RZZ JPY

_____

ZVLY VJ NBFFAHJN.

_____

—EPVYL NYRJJZY   _____

Puzzle 7-23 *answers on page 261*

MQAU ECU VGPHHUH HCODQNV EUNJUG

RPTUH EO UPTC OECUG, ECZH HCOZMJ

DUJO, ROG ECQH DPH ECU DQHC OR ECU

VGPNJRPECUGH OR ECU DOGMJ.

—FMPTA UMA

THE BIBLE

Puzzle 7-24 *answers on page 261*

MTO XCYN MGIQO RQGPT UTLCNT JTP, OQWO

_____

OQTX JWX RTT XCYN ICCZ BCNSR, WPZ

_____

IMCNGLX XCYN LWOQTN BQGAQ GR GP QTWVTP.

_____

Puzzle 7-25 *answers on page 262*

AD KDV YDFWBV VD BKVBFVIJK UVFIKWBFU,

_____

YDF ZE UD ADJKW UDNB GIPB TKOJVVJKWSE

_____

BKVBFVIJKBA IKWBSU.

_____

NEPWPLIWP KP OI GIN FIHP EPAWN. PZPG

_____

NEIMVE IMW IMNKAWO RAG UH BPWUHEUGV,

_____

JPN NEP UGKAWO RAG UH QPUGV WPGPKPO

_____

OAJ QJ OAJ.

_____

KFFPYVMQEVV YV XFUQA YQ WME MELGW

_____

FK L SMYPA; XUW WME GFA FK SFGGESWYFQ

_____

VMLPP AGYHE YW KLG KGFO MYO.

_____

Puzzle 7-28 *answers on page 262*

KDGTG HA BCKDHBP QGKKGT JCT U SUB,

KDUB KDUK DG ADCMWF GUK UBF FTHBR,

UBF KDUK DG ADCMWF SURG DHA ACMW

GBYCN PCCF HB DHA WUQCT.

Puzzle 7-29 *answers on page 262*

NSIXUGJI, CZPW YZSL HQPWI, OSIM UI

ANLQIM UCIZ CZPWJ MNW ANSLAN UGJ

KUPW NQBIWCF SV FZL NWL.

THE KORAN

Puzzle 7-30 *answers on page 262*

BGL GL ZBM FGJPYUN US ZBM BMHQMJL

_____

HJY ZBM MHIZB. BM UIYHGJL CGSM HJY

_____

YMHZB HJY BHL XUEMI UQMI HCC ZBGJPL.

_____

Puzzle 7-31 *answers on page 262*

ZBBLHM PFHKBZHBVS BF YNZSLNK ZHM BF

_____

BCL DOMMVL YNZSLN ZHM KBZHM UY

_____

BNUVS FWLMOLHB BF ZVVZC.

_____

BP LZRP WZSP FQI Z AITK DZKOQD, TQ KLZK

FQI WZF KPTKOUF ZYZODTK WZDNODS ZDS

KLZK FQIH QBD ZEQTKMP WZF KPTKOUF

ZYZODTK FQI.

JFN CNUNW FNIUNWC, JFN NIMJF, IWB

IDD EFX BENDD OW JFNL ROUN RDXMQ

JX FOL. IDD SMNIJYMNC SNDNHMIJN FOC

KMIOCNC. QNJ QXY SIWWXJ YWBNMCJIWB

JFNOM KMIOCNC. HNWORWIWJ OC

FN IWB PXMROUOWR.

Puzzle 7-34 *answers on page 263*

OMXJGM HXMMAGL SL IXBY CXJ ET FTV,

_____

YXLEAPF DMAPFL SL ET EIG VTTM TY IAL

_____

OXBXHG, XPV XBWL-FAKAPF OMTHSMG

_____

L SL XVWALLATP.

_____

THE TALMUD

Puzzle 7-35 *answers on page 263*

T CPWTL YFODF OJ XAI OXIWPBPWIWC OJ

_____

ZOEW T ZWIIWP YFODF OJ XAI PWTC.

_____

Puzzle 7-36 *answers on page 263*

ZIS PSRQME VXDM XE WKEIMN ATQO AB VXDM;

_____

ZIS BXMJNE VS VXDM, PXFNE VXDM SF IXE EXNM.

_____

Puzzle 7-37 *answers on page 263*

UBPIFIG JILEGPKL D LRVOYI YRSI RL DL

_____

OXRYEK DL EBPXOB BI BDJ JILEGPKIJ EBI

_____

IVERGI UPGYJ; DVJ UBPIFIG GILZXIL D LRVOYI

_____

YRSI IDGVL DL AXZB AIGRE DL EBPXOB BI

_____

BDJ GILZXIJ EBI IVERGI UPGYJ.

_____

HINTS

Puzzle 7-1: The word "type" is found in this puzzle.

Puzzle 7-2: The word "belief" is found in this puzzle.

Puzzle 7-3: The word "saints" is found in this puzzle.

Puzzle 7-4: The word "style" is found in this puzzle.

Puzzle 7-5: The word "worship" is found in this puzzle.

Puzzle 7-6: The word "positive" is found in this puzzle.

Puzzle 7-7: The word "idea" is found in this puzzle.

Puzzle 7-8: The word "envy" is found in this puzzle.

Puzzle 7-9: The word "idle" is found in this puzzle.

Puzzle 7-10: The word "heal" is found in this puzzle.

Puzzle 7-11: The word "meal" is found in this puzzle.

Puzzle 7-12: The word "spoon" is found in this puzzle.

Puzzle 7-13: The word "coal" is found in this puzzle.

Puzzle 7-14: The word "virtue" is found in this puzzle.

Puzzle 7-15: The word "nothing" is found in this puzzle.

Puzzle 7-16: The word "glory" is found in this puzzle.

Puzzle 7-17: The word "done" is found in this puzzle.

Puzzle 7-18: The word "worth" is found in this puzzle.

Puzzle 7-19: The word "books" is found in this puzzle.

Puzzle 7-20: The word "eagle" is found in this puzzle.

Puzzle 7-21: The word "smile" is found in this puzzle.

Puzzle 7-22: The word "breath" is found in this puzzle.

Puzzle 7-23: The word "faces" is found in this puzzle.

Puzzle 7-24: The word "shine" is found in this puzzle.

Puzzle 7-25: The word "angels" is found in this puzzle.

Puzzle 7-26: The word "heart" is found in this puzzle.

Puzzle 7-27: The word "child" is found in this puzzle.

Puzzle 7-28: The word "labor" is found in this puzzle.

Puzzle 7-29: The word "church" is found in this puzzle.

Puzzle 7-30: The word "power" is found in this puzzle.

Puzzle 7-31: The word "attend" is found in this puzzle.

Puzzle 7-32: The word "nation" is found in this puzzle.

Puzzle 7-33: The word "dwell" is found in this puzzle.

Puzzle 7-34: The word "palace" is found in this puzzle.

Puzzle 7-35: The word "dream" is found in this puzzle.

Puzzle 7-36: The word "time" is found in this puzzle.

Puzzle 7-37: The word "merit" is found in this puzzle.

CHAPTER 8

Scientific Discoveries

Where in the world would we be without science? What we think of as "science" is actually made up of many fields of study that includes biology, chemistry, physics, and mathematics. Within these fields you'll find research that has been or is being performed to explore and explain everything from the secrets of the universe to the best way to keep your breakfast cereal crunchy in milk. In this chapter you'll find quotations about the various areas of scientific study as well as statements from famous scientists about their work and viewpoints.

THE STUDY OF LIFE

Puzzle 8-1 *answers on page 264*

JM ZKP IRWBJBSH AY YSBAWPD JMDJBJDRSHI

_____

SMD WSXPI, DRWJMQ ZKP XAMIZSMZHN-

_____

WPXRWWJMQ IZWRQQHP YAW POJIZPMXP,

_____

EP IPP S LAEPWYRH SMD PBPW-SXZJMQ

_____

YAWF AY IPHPXZJAM.

_____

—XKSWHPI DSWEJM _____

Puzzle 8-2 *answers on page 264*

MYOUKYU IPM GVHHX AODIHZD PKS

_____

YUVDPOKDS. YVUPDOHKOMDM IPTU

_____

YUVDPOKDS AODIHZD PKS GVHHX.

_____

—PMIWUS NHKDPQZU _____

Puzzle 8-3 *answers on page 264*

EPV VUUVTNV DR IBRV BU UELEBUEBNLI

_____

BZOHDALABIBES DT L NDIDUULI UNLIV.

_____

—HBNPLHW WLMFBTU _____

I OHPC JHVVCZ NOIA MEIBJIMVC, QU ROIJO

_____

CHJO AVIGON PHEIHNIWB, IT YACTYV,

_____

IA MECACEPCZ, QU NOC NCEX

_____

BHNYEHV ACVCJNIWB.

_____

—JOHEVCA ZHERIB _____

Puzzle 8-5 *answers on page 264*

RO ZHZFW PEUUYFEGU YZTJXTOJ, RO ZHZFW

_____

KEFHROB VZTKY, RO ZHZFW BFTRO PL GTOJ

_____

UYZFZ RG T GUPFW PL UYZ ZTFUY.

_____

—FTKYZX KTFGPO _____

CHEMICAL PROPERTIES

Puzzle 8-6 *answers on page 264*

N PTKTQOZR PTVY ODVO ZAIT NB TQONPTZR

_____

V SVOOTP AU KDTSNBOPR. ODVO SFBO

_____

GT JDR SR JNUT OPTVOB ST ZNET OALNK JVBOT.

_____

—YVINY GNBBAQTOOT _____

Puzzle 8-7 *answers on page 265*

KYS OY SYKK NBQ SGY CYAJYS SGFS GFC

KYR OY SB ON EBFK: ON CSJYVESG KPYC

CBKYKN PV ON SYVFAPSN.

—KBQPC HFCSYQJ _____

Puzzle 8-8 *answers on page 265*

SII JMWHLWJTOSI OMWPTXJLN TX LWSIIN

YMNXTOX; SBQ SII JMWHLWJTOSI

OMWPTXJX EBHU TJ.

—LTOMSLQ Y. VWNBPSB

Puzzle 8-9 *answers on page 265*

A VEZ DETSFD DFED DFB VEI RL JURSUBZZ

_____

AZ PBADFBU ZVALD PRU BEZI.

_____

—WEUAB XTUAB _____

Puzzle 8-10 *answers on page 265*

CXQRKAD DITBAZJXF AZ JIT DITBAZJXF CL

_____

DRXWCK DCBOCYKNZ. WACDITBAZJXF AZ

_____

JIT ZJYNF CL DRXWCK DCBOCYKNZ JIRJ DXRMU.

_____

—BAST RNRBZ _____

Puzzle 8-11 *answers on page 265*

WSD UDFOQOWOBQ BF OQVAQOWG OV

_____

UBOQY WSD VALD WSOQY BZDK AQU BZDK

_____

AQU DIRDPWOQY UOFFDKDQW KDVEJWV.

_____

—MDQNALOQ FKAQTJOQ _____

Puzzle 8-12 *answers on page 265*

DAJOJ TU XHDATXW TX Y KYDJOMTCCYO DAYD

_____

DJCCU QHI TD'U WHTXW DH SJ Y SIDDJOECQ.

_____

—OTKAYOG SIKBPTXUDJO EICCJO

_____

Puzzle 8-13 *answers on page 265*

MAH AUVCP YZCKP VUXM TIPMKPUH MI

_____

BZCVH MAH GZIYNHVX BIZ MAH HNHTMZIPKT

_____

VCTAKPH MI XINOH.

_____

—JCOKJ XCZPIBB _____

ZK CKMRKSET QZCIY KCKR GPKATRA ZKA

_____

KCKRSD-KCKR SCURY, ZKA CQ GR YPBBRRAY

_____

EKBR, GR'Y CK. GR STRZSY GCY QZCI

_____

PTRY YCUFID ZY FTZBSCBR YGESY.

_____

—BGZTIRY Q. WRSSRTCKN

_____

Puzzle 8-15 *answers on page 266*

ZU GI DRR GBJWIE BT ASI DOOXVQAZBT ASDA

_____

GSDA ZO DNNIQAIE DO AJXI ZO JIDRRC AJXI,

_____

ASIJI GBXRE KI RZAARI SBQI BU DELDTNI.

_____

—BJLZRRI GJZYSA _____

Puzzle 8-16 *answers on page 266*

ZSOULDSK ULZU RPS'U EWGG, D IPS'U

_____

RZSU UP DSQWSU. DUE EZGW DE MCPPX

_____

PX NUDGDUO, ZSI NUDGDUO DE ENAAWEE.

_____

—ULPVZE Z. WIDEPS _____

PLAYING WITH NUMBERS

Puzzle 8-17 *answers on page 266*

XAVIOXAVLRH LH A DAXO ZFABOQ

_____

ARRJUQLYD VJ ROUVALY HLXZFO UEFOH

_____

GLVI XOAYLYDFOHH XAUMH JY ZAZOU.

_____

—QAPLQ ILFWOUV _____

Puzzle 8-18 *answers on page 266*

KSHRYKSHTMP TP HRY SQH EJ OTFTVO HRY

_____

PSKY VSKY HE UTJJYQYVH HRTVOP.

_____

—IGLYP RYVQTWETVMSQY

_____

Puzzle 8-19 *answers on page 266*

I PIQOKPIQGYGIV'Z FKJEQIQGAV FKZQZ AV

_____

QOK VEPRKF AN RIU JFAANZ OK OIZ BGSKV.

_____

—I. Z. RKZGYASGYO _____

Puzzle 8-20 *answers on page 266*

JWPTDTUW JIFWC HWKHGW TGG, JINQWJINTDC

_____

JIFW NQWJ CIP, IUP NQWKGKSZ JIFWC

_____

NQWJ CTUMAG.

_____

—JIBNTU GANQWB _____

RWGD FU XGC FC CGDIPH? CQDWFCZ FC

_____

PHKGDFQC DQ DWH FCAFCFDH, GKK FC

_____

PHKGDFQC DQ CQDWFCZ, G XHGC EHDRHHC

_____

CQDWFCZ GCB HMHPYDWFCZ.

_____

—EKGFUH SGUOGK _____

PHYSICS AND THE UNIVERSE

Puzzle 8-22 *answers on page 267*

QDRNR FO JYQ QDR OZFVDQROQ FJBFHWQFYJ

_____

QDWQ RJRNVE AFZZ RKRN IR YIQWFJWIZR

_____

GNYC QDR WQYC.

_____

—WZIRNQ RFJOQRFJ _____

Puzzle 8-23 *answers on page 267*

BR XPT YBZG WP SOFC ON OHHDC HBC

_____

WLTDX RLPS ZJLOWJG, XPT STZW RBLZW

_____

BNUCNW WGC TNBUCLZC.

_____

—JOLD ZOION _____

EA BWLU CX XCEFUY. CO CX QWEFUYOY

_____

JVDYHXOLVDCVB WN OZY JVCGYHXY, MZA

_____

CO CX LX CO CX LVD MZA CO YPCXOX LO LUU.

_____

—XOYFZYV ZLMSCVB _____

LCTAV OCT XQV HTL ACTBIVK OCVH LCVE

_____

GZQAL BTUV XBQTAA JDXHLDU UVBCXHZBA

_____

BXHHTL YTAAZPSE CXRV DHKVQALTTK ZL.

_____

—HZVSA PTCQ _____

Puzzle 8-26 *answers on page 267*

GXX FV DUOLHPL HL WHTUWY HJDFLLHNXW

_____

FY TYHAHGX. HT HL HJDFLLHNXW SZTHX

_____

OFS SZIWYLTGZI HT, GZI TUWZ HT NWPFJWL

_____

TYHAHGX.

_____

—WYZWLT YSTUWYVFYI _____

Puzzle 8-27 *answers on page 267*

DAHAEDTL WH RCDPEVWSAN TFDWCHWMQ.

_____

WM WH BCXWJY EJN BDQWJY KWML E BFDBCHA.

_____

—SCDE JAEVA LFDHMCJ

_____

DOING RESEARCH

Puzzle 8-28 *answers on page 268*

LTDHQUH QHR'O G APVQNQYR. QW QO KPAP, KP'Z

_____

TGIP G FEUT PGHQPA OQFP AGQHQRN FYRPD.

_____

—VPYR VPZPAFGR _____

Puzzle 8-29 *answers on page 268*

TMYMETBL JY ULM ETU CF YMMJVN OLEU

_____

MQMTXCVM MKYM LEY YMMV, EVR RCJVN

_____

OLEU VC CVM MKYM LEY RCVM.

_____

—EVCVXSCAY _____

AE AV F GXXB TXMRARG KNKMHAVK DXM

_____

F MKVKFMHZ VHAKREAVE EX BAVHFMB

_____

F YKE ZQYXEZKVAV KLKMQ BFQ CKDXMK

_____

CMKFIDFVE AE IKKYV ZAT QXSRG.

_____

—IXRMFB JXMKRU   _____

WAD WZVKSOD BNWA ZDFDJZMA NF WAJW NW

_____

WDOOF GVK BAJW PDVPOD BDZD WANUINUE

_____

JSVKW GDFWDZTJG, UVW WVHVZZVB. NW'F

_____

ONID TZNCNUE J MJZ KFNUE J ZDJZCNDB HNZZVZ.

_____

—SDZUJZT OVVHNF _____

HINTS

Puzzle 8-1: The word "races" is found in this puzzle.

Puzzle 8-2: The word "proof" is found in this puzzle.

Puzzle 8-3: The word "life" is found in this puzzle.

Puzzle 8-4: The word "slight" is found in this puzzle.

Puzzle 8-5: The word "beach" is found in this puzzle.

Puzzle 8-6: The word "love" is found in this puzzle.

Puzzle 8-7: The word "goal" is found in this puzzle.

Puzzle 8-8: The word "know" is found in this puzzle.

Puzzle 8-9: The word "swift" is found in this puzzle.

Puzzle 8-10: The word "study" is found in this puzzle.

Puzzle 8-11: The word "same" is found in this puzzle.

Puzzle 8-12: The word "nothing" is found in this puzzle.

Puzzle 8-13: The word "frame" is found in this puzzle.

Puzzle 8-14: The word "fails" is found in this puzzle.

Puzzle 8-15: The word "true" is found in this puzzle.

Puzzle 8-16: The word "utility" is found in this puzzle.

Puzzle 8-17: The word "marks" is found in this puzzle.

Puzzle 8-18: The word "name" is found in this puzzle.

Puzzle 8-19: The word "rests" is found in this puzzle.

Puzzle 8-20: The word "makes" is found in this puzzle.

Puzzle 8-21: The word "mean" is found in this puzzle.

Puzzle 8-22: The word "atom" is found in this puzzle.

Puzzle 8-23: The word "truly" is found in this puzzle.

Puzzle 8-24: The word "exists" is found in this puzzle.

Puzzle 8-25: The word "first" is found in this puzzle.

Puzzle 8-26: The word "until" is found in this puzzle.

Puzzle 8-27: The word "prying" is found in this puzzle.

Puzzle 8-28: The word "time" is found in this puzzle.

Puzzle 8-29: The word "art" is found in this puzzle.

Puzzle 8-30: The word "young" is found in this puzzle.

Puzzle 8-31: The word "mirror" is found in this puzzle.

CHAPTER 9

Playing Sports

Sports are a great way to blow off steam, build and maintain your competitive spirit, and work on developing your physical skills. There are many different ways you can lead a sporting life: you can take lessons, join a team, play with your children, watch an event on TV, join a crowd at a stadium, or even bet on the outcome (in states where gambling is legal, of course)! The puzzles you'll be solving in this chapter will give you insight and tips into the worlds of baseball, basketball, football, golf, hockey, and tennis.

BASEBALL

Puzzle 9-1 *answers on page 268*

BYH EOKRN D LYYN OTKQK YC BYHU FTCK

_____

LUTOOTRL D JDEKJDFF, DRN TS SHURE YHS TS

_____

PDE SZK YSZKU PDB DUYHRN DFF SZK STVK.

_____

—WTV JYHSYR _____

Puzzle 9-2 *answers on page 268*

AT AF ECBCG'F THB JMXCJMDD, OMGQ NAPX

_____

EHRDPG'F NGHE ELMF M OADDAHGMABC

_____

DHHNCP DANC.

_____

—VLQDDAX PADDCB _____

Puzzle 9-3 *answers on page 269*

COG OPQRGFC COYBZ CH RH YB LPFGLPMM

_____

YF CH OYC P QHTBR LPFGLPMM JYCO P

_____

QHTBR LPC, FVTPQGMK.

_____

—CGR JYMMYPDF _____

Puzzle 9-4 *answers on page 269*

X ETDTU SNUTK ME XHHTYMH IXSLN. SNT

_____

SUCAZHT XR, CELT XE M KNXHT X SCRR

_____

CET SNMS MXE'S ETDTU ZTTE RTTE

_____

ZW SNXR YTETUMSXCE.

_____

—RMSLNT IMXYT _____

BASKETBALL

Puzzle 9-5 *answers on page 269*

Y SLXLQ OJJULD VZ ZNL BJSELGHLSBLE JF

_____

AYEEYSK V WYK ENJZ . . . INLS TJH ZNYSU

_____

VWJHZ ZNL BJSELGHLSBLE TJH VOIVTE

_____

ZNYSU JF V SLKVZYXL QLEHOZ.

_____

—AYBNVLO RJQDVS _____

Puzzle 9-6 *answers on page 269*

DRWE SPE DRPD OUBUIE GS JWLCWAD.

_____

DRWO DRWE DWQQ EUZ JLPADGAW VPXWS

_____

JWLCWAD. G NGSR DRWE'I VPXW ZJ

_____

DRWGL VGOIS.

_____

—NGQD ARPVBWLQPGO _____

Puzzle 9-7 *answers on page 269*

IZZF, NACCAS, NAYC. RAMAS DAC GC SAYC.

_____

TRCGD JZTS IZZF GY NACCAS PRF JZTS

_____

NACCAS GY NAYC.

_____

—CGH FTRWPR _____

Puzzle 9-8 *answers on page 269*

XIN XEATKQXI HFN QXI HA X HXWRAJHXSS

_____

WJXT KG BA PTFLW DC, DC, DC.

_____

—HKSS ZXDPBI _____

Puzzle 9-9 *answers on page 269*

H IAWIQV AIPLN WNEM OEZOAE IVS BE

_____

IRZPG CERZPMDHML GEJNMHXPEV. H'KE LZG

_____

I GEJNMHXPE. HG'V JIAAED YPVG LZ LEG

_____

GNE DIBM RIAA.

_____

—JNICAEV RICSAEQ _____

FOOTBALL

Puzzle 9-10 *answers on page 270*

N ODFNDAD ZJD XSED NW MDWNXBDM ZI

_____

QDVSQM ZJD IBDW VJI JNZ ZJD JSQMDWZ.

_____

NR HIT USB'Z ZSYD NZ, HIT WJITFMB'Z LFSH.

_____

—PSUY FSEODQZ _____

Puzzle 9-11 *answers on page 270*

KSQGXGJH GH QGPT YSSXUAQQ; GY WSM

_____

HTT NAWQGIOX, IS XOFSMIO XOT OSQT.

_____

—VSOE Y. PTEETNW _____

UC K SKT RKXHVNZ XVINN CGGXEKAA

YKSNZ UT K IGR, VN ZVGQAP EN PNHAKINP

ANYKAAM PNKP.

—NISK EGSENHJ

LU QRG HCB VXXZ QRGM SXCE ISXB COO

CKRGW QRG CMX ORTLBP WSXLMT, QRG'MX

CW WSX IMRBP XBE RU WSX URRWKCOO ZLWHS.

—KLOO FGBMR

RNNEGQAA GZWIYF NUE EVT FNMWNANYWFE

_____

EVQE AUZHF WI FNXT NEVTZCWFT

_____

ZTFKTMEQGAT MWEWDTIF. EVTO FQO

_____

RNNEGQAA WF Q XTEQKVNZ RNZ

_____

QXTZWMQ'F FWIRUAITFF.

_____

—YTNZYT R. CWAA _____

GOLF

PYVD UR G PGQK UN ECUIC G OGVV—

_____

YNK GNL G CGVD UNICKR UN LUGQKTKW—

_____

UR BVGIKL YN G OGVV—KUPCT TCYFRGNL

_____

QUVKR UN LUGQKTKW. TCK YOXKIT OKUNP

_____

TY CUT TCK RQGVV OGVV OFT NYT

_____

TCK VGWPKW.

_____

—XYCN IFNNUNPCGQ _____

RE FWI HYS KWRXK ZW ZMYWD H OLIG, RZ

_____

RV RUJWYZHXZ ZW ZMYWD RZ HMSHA WE

_____

FWI, AWDX ZMS EHRYDHF, VW FWI AWX'Z

_____

DHVZS SXSYKF KWRXK GHON ZW JRON RZ IJ.

_____

—ZWUUF GWLZ _____

Puzzle 9-17 *answers on page 271*

DZ D'I LM HSW FLXOPW NME TDGSHMDMG

_____

PHNOHP, D GWH DMPDEW ZNPH. DZ GLE

_____

VNMHP HL KTNJ HSOLXGS, TWH SDI.

_____

—RLR SLKW _____

Puzzle 9-18 *answers on page 271*

C'Y CA BNS DQQKU UQ YOZN C ZJA BSRR

_____

WQO DNCZN LRJABU JPS SKCHRS.

_____

—RSS BPSECAQ _____

Puzzle 9-19 *answers on page 271*

FBB FLB AHII LTOL. ABJHQWB YBHNW RZ

_____

BVDBNTBUJB LHXB WLRGU KB FLHF HTN

_____

RZZBNW IBWW NBWTWFHUJB FLHU ETNF.

_____

—MHJSUTJS IHQW _____

Puzzle 9-20 *answers on page 271*

G ZRH R PKOHAVNWI ACBAVGAOUA KO JZA SKIN

_____

UKWVDA JKHRY. G ZRH R ZKIA GO OKJZGOS.

_____

TGDDAH JZA FRII ROH DROX JZA HGLKJ.

_____

—HKO RHRTD _____

HOCKEY

Puzzle 9-21 *answers on page 271*

KC'Y VRC ZNR ZKVY CNE UKJNC CNAC'Y

_____

KGBRWCAVC, KC'Y XEKVJ ZKMMKVJ CR

_____

UKJNC. KU SRF JEC PNAMMEVJET AVT

_____

WEVEJE, EOEWSRVE ZAVCY CR CAQE A

_____

 YNRC AC SRF.

_____

—XAWPMAS BMAJEW   _____

Puzzle 9-22 *answers on page 271*

M TOFW AJ M CMNE NOQQGN EAJF DCMD

_____

CXFWGZ TPMZGNJ JDNAWG YCGU DCGZ

_____

FMU'D CAD XUG MUXDCGN.

_____

—SAIIZ FMUUXU _____

Puzzle 9-23 *answers on page 272*

CA PAN FEOA UERO BXX NJA NHMA HF NJA

_____

FJX, BFW CA WEF'N AKAF JBKA NE PE

_____

NE NJA JEOYHNBX.

_____

—RZBW YBZT _____

Puzzle 9-24 *answers on page 272*

RH BFZH BAH UAWNBHUB NWPBH BW BAH

_____

TPQZ FEY FNNOKH OE ODD APSWN.

_____

—IWIIJ QDFNZH _____

Puzzle 9-25 *answers on page 272*

P XAPUEY GZJD KE PKAE DQ JNPDE, RPFE

_____

RQHNEU JEOJE, KE PKAE DQ JRQQD—

_____

OQD OEHEJJPYMAU PKAE DQ JHQYE— POL

_____

RPFE LYMFE.

_____

—XMEYYE XPWE _____

TENNIS

Puzzle 9-26 *answers on page 272*

FEY'UZ SET TE TVIZ TOZ MWMTMVTMUZ

_____

VWK CNVF FEYB SVRZ. MW V KZGMDMUZ

_____

DZT, GEWLMKZWGZ MD TOZ KMLLZBZWGZ.

_____

—GOBMD ZUZBT _____

Puzzle 9-27 *answers on page 272*

OLM NVZ VRXLBY IVYNS V NLMGRJ GRVO

_____

XHUJA ALMFRJB VZA PZLI ISJYSJK YSJO

_____

BSLMRA BYVO YLWJYSJK.

_____

—AK. SJKFJKY SJZAHZ _____

Puzzle 9-28 *answers on page 272*

CUV CNFIPXV GACU BV AK CUDC VOVNJ

_____

BDCTU A SXDJ DLDAWKC YAOV FSSFWVWCK:

_____

IBSANV, TNFGH, PDXX PFJK, TFINC, DWH BJKVXY.

_____

—LFNDW AODWAKVOAT _____

Puzzle 9-29 *answers on page 272*

LV SYMEBJTCE MLAATOP ILBBTEZ NSDAOE

_____

ILP YDBV L ITKEZ ZSDGOEC RLIE TVYS L

_____

CNEVE XBSI JMS'C LXBLTZ SX WTBRTVTL JSSOX.

_____

—BSZ OLWEB _____

HINTS

Puzzle 9-1: The word "life" is found in this puzzle.

Puzzle 9-2: The word "kids" is found in this puzzle.

Puzzle 9-3: The word "round" is found in this puzzle.

Puzzle 9-4: The word "toss" is found in this puzzle.

Puzzle 9-5: The word "shot" is found in this puzzle.

Puzzle 9-6: The word "minds" is found in this puzzle.

Puzzle 9-7: The word "best" is found in this puzzle.

Puzzle 9-8: The word "star" is found in this puzzle.

Puzzle 9-9: The word "laugh" is found in this puzzle.

Puzzle 9-10: The word "game" is found in this puzzle.

Puzzle 9-11: The word "hole" is found in this puzzle.

Puzzle 9-12: The word "games" is found in this puzzle.

Puzzle 9-13: The word "wrong" is found in this puzzle.

Puzzle 9-14: The word "lurks" is found in this puzzle.

Puzzle 9-15: The word "small" is found in this puzzle.

Puzzle 9-16: The word "throw" is found in this puzzle.

Puzzle 9-17: The word "starts" is found in this puzzle.

Puzzle 9-18: The word "plants" is found in this puzzle.

Puzzle 9-19: The word "high" is found in this puzzle.

Puzzle 9-20: The word "course" is found in this puzzle.

Puzzle 9-21: The word "wins" is found in this puzzle.

Puzzle 9-22: The word "disc" is found in this puzzle.

Puzzle 9-23: The word "nose" is found in this puzzle.

Puzzle 9-24: The word "route" is found in this puzzle.

Puzzle 9-25: The word "skate" is found in this puzzle.

Puzzle 9-26: The word "your" is found in this puzzle.

Puzzle 9-27: The word "couple" is found in this puzzle.

Puzzle 9-28: The word "match" is found in this puzzle.

Puzzle 9-29: The word "scene" is found in this puzzle.

CHAPTER 10

Cryptogram Jumble

This final chapter is packed with great quotes from an eclectic group. Some of the puzzles are inspirational, some are funny, and some are a bit bizarre—but all are interesting! You'll gain insight from some of the world's most famous writers, actors, athletes, politicians, scientists, and comedians. So get your mind moving while decoding these attention-grabbing puzzles, and enjoy this last chapter!

NJP IYKTVPU MW DKN NJRN NJPYP RYP

_____

IYKTVPUW. NJP IYKTVPU MW PHIPGNMDB

_____

KNJPYXMWP RDE NJMDAMDB NJRN JRQMDB

_____

IYKTVPUW MW R IYKTVPU.

_____

—NJPKEKYP YOTMD _____

Puzzle 10-2 *answers on page 273*

YGYCS IBQMT QV XH XCEQVE. EBY RCKUMYW

_____

QV BKO EK CYWXQH XH XCEQVE KHIY

_____

BY FCKOV AR.

_____

—RXUMK RQIXVVK _____

Puzzle 10-3 *answers on page 273*

BODKOJRR QAYQUR XISDASJR OXRV; UDM

_____

PQI'C RCJQA RJPDIZ NQRJ QIZ VJJB UDMO

_____

LDDC DI LXORC NQRJ.

_____

—LOJZJOXPV YXAPDF _____

Puzzle 10-4 *answers on page 273*

WVX'UB HBJBU SI KVVN SI BJBUWVHB ABRRI

WVX ZEBH WVX ZOH, SHN WVX'UB HBJBU

SI CSN SI AEBW ISW ZEBH WVX RVIB.

—RVX EVRAM

Puzzle 10-5 *answers on page 273*

GDO WUYNKOIH GDTG OFCHG CV GDO

MYUKE GYETQ RTVVYG NO HYKXOE NQ

GDO KOXOK YS GDCVPCVB GDTG RUOTGOE GDOI.

—TKNOUG OCVHGOCV

VCECO ABZXR RLWR W FDWMM SOBZQ BT

_____

RLBZSLRTZM GBDDJRRCA QCBQMC GWV

_____

GLWVSC RLC YBOMA: JVACCA JR'F RLC

_____

BVMP RLJVS RLWR CECO LWF!

_____

—DWOSWOCR DCWAC _____

Puzzle 10-7 *answers on page 274*

BVKVKOVB UZFFGEVTT CAVTE'M CVFVEC

_____

YFAE RUA DAY ZBV AB RUZM DAY UZLV;

_____

GM CVFVECT TAXVXD AE RUZM DAY MUGEI.

_____

—CZXV QZBEVJGV

Puzzle 10-8 *answers on page 274*

SZASNM BJXJXVJB, IULJBM XSN LSUJ NID.

_____

VDU ULIMJ ALI LSUJ NID OIQ'U AGQ DQZJMM

_____

NID LSUJ ULJX. SQO ULJQ NID OJMUBIN

_____

NIDBMJZH.

_____

—BGPLSBO X. QGFIQ _____

Puzzle 10-9 *answers on page 274*

J VNJTG VNUV BPWBRP QUTV BPUDP

_____

MW XYDN VNUV WTP WK VNPMP AUFM

_____

ZWSPCTXPTVM NUA LPVVPC ZPV WYV WK

_____

VNP QUF UTA RPV VNPX NUSP JV.

_____

—AQJZNV A. PJMPTNWQPC

_____

VADUDSXX AD PCZUX TZSJMSX TCDHAUSDTS.

_____

VADUDSXX AD MWADVADF TZSJMSX

_____

LZCHCKDUDSXX. VADUDSXX AD FAQADF

_____

TZSJMSX ICQS.

_____

—IJC MOK _____

Puzzle 10-11 *answers on page 274*

PNIQ LYQ Y HIGLVK KIIEL UBLP PNGII PNJKXL

_____

PV TI PGBOQ NYHHQ JK PNJL MVGOE:

_____

LVZIVKI PV OVFI, LVZIPNJKX PV EV, YKE

_____

LVZIPNJKX PV NVHI CVG.

_____

—PVZ TVEIPP _____

Puzzle 10-12 *answers on page 275*

J UA HBFHUBFC YX CJF, QEY YSFBF JW

_____

TX GUEWF LXB KSJGS J UA HBFHUBFC YX VJPP.

_____

—AUSUYAU OUTCSJ _____

Puzzle 10-13 *answers on page 275*

INOG TGP KZYJ VGXZHOG KMGA MZLG

_____

OETGKMNPR KE OZA; CEEYO, VGXZHOG

_____

KMGA MZLG KE OZA OETGKMNPR.

_____

—SYZKE   _____

Puzzle 10-14 *answers on page 275*

KNP YPRK FBV KZ UNPPT VZMTRPES QR

_____

KZ KTV KZ UNPPT RZHPZOP PERP MJ.

_____

—HBTI KFBQO   _____

BRCT GZN RQSC MZTHPICTMC, GZN MQT

_____

RQSC Q JZE ZH HNT. QTI BRCT GZN RQSC

_____

HNT, GZN MQT IZ QOQFPTV ERPTVK.

_____

—YZC TQOQER _____

TK BOS TW XQWCSY BK BOS CGTOR QOZ

_____

POZSYWCQOZW BOS CGTOR JSFF, BOS

_____

GQW QC CGS WQXS CTXS, TOWTRGC TOCB

_____

QOZ POZSYWCQOZTOR BK XQOL CGTORW.

_____

—ITOASOC IQO RBRG _____

Puzzle 10-17 *answers on page 275*

N IWF SBM DWCT YBST VDTKT N NSMTSGTG

_____

MB YB, JLM N MDNSE N DWCT TSGTG LX

_____

VDTKT N NSMTSGTG MB JT.

_____

—GBLYRWH WGWIH

_____

Puzzle 10-18 *answers on page 275*

NUQ ZWL XKHZUPRM FUMR WCUQB W

_____

ARMHUL KL WL EUQM UT AVWN BEWL KL

_____

W NRWM UT ZULPRMHWBKUL.

_____

—AVWBU

G BVNR QTHWF DBR PRYD IVO DT SGNR

VFNGXR DT OTHM XBGAFMRW GY DT QGWF

THD IBVD DBRO IVWD VWF DBRW VFNGYR

DBRC DT FT GD.

—BVMMO Y. DMHCVW

UGL KYYA FLYFSL XSLLF TDZG NLUULO CU

_____

IPKGU UGCI UGL NCA FLYFSL. YQ ZYDOXL,

_____

UGL NCA FLYFSL LIRYV UGL MCEPIK

_____

GYDOX TDZG TYOL.

_____

—MYYAV CSSLI _____

Puzzle 10-21 *answers on page 276*

DFEWQ DLR ZRWG DRCD FI TFNRZ XC

_____

VFD HWTWHXDQ DF BWOR NWZ YPD DLR

_____

HWTWHXDQ DF TZRMRVD XD.

_____

—WVVR F'LWZR BHHFZBXHO _____

_____

Puzzle 10-22 *answers on page 276*

NI BKI ACBSIJ YG ETK FCETDCFA; NI YIZERI

_____

NCBF NI FCPLH. NCIL FCI RPLJ PA STKI, XEG

_____

QEVVENA VPHI B ACBJEN FCBF LIUIK VIBUIA.

_____

—YTJJCB _____

KWMYSMYZ MU KWA AYAEX NC BFAJKMOMKX.

_____

MK'U UAGC-BNYUBMNIU, JYR JYXKWMYZ

_____

UAGC-BNYUBMNIU MU GNIUX. XNI BJY'K

_____

KFX KN RN KWMYZU. XNI UMETGX

_____

EIUK RN KWMYZU.

_____

—FJX HFJRHIFX _____

MGN RNMHNKQQ WQ W FWAPMF EWF CK

_____

FM QJPZAKN ALWF MGN RNMHNKQQ PF

_____

KXGEWAPMF. ALK LGSWF SPFX PQ MGN

_____

ZGFXWSKFAWI NKQMGNEK.

_____

—VMLF Z. UKFFKXT _____

UYN MPVVNHNDEN ANUFNND UYN HPQYU

_____

FIHM KDM UYN KTSILU HPQYU FIHM PL

_____

UYN MPVVNHNDEN ANUFNND TPQYUDPDQ

_____

KDM K TPQYUDPDQ AOQ.

_____

—SKHW UFKPD _____

Puzzle 10-26 *answers on page 277*

S UHXXHV XYMOSTF OASO BFHBEF XSTF CAFV

_____

OLZYVP OH JFMYPV MHXFOAYVP UHXBEFOFEZ

_____

QHHEBLHHQ YM OH RVJFLFMOYXSOF OAF

_____

YVPFVRYOZ HQ UHXBEFOF QHHEM.

_____

—JHRPESM SJSXM _____

Puzzle 10-27 *answers on page 277*

ICH VDDVIHKTIH LP ICH PQIQKH NVDD FLI

_____

EH ICH JHKULF NCL RTFFLI KHTX. VI NVDD

_____

EH ICH JHKULF NCL XLHU FLI OFLN CLN IL DHTKF.

_____

—TDGVF ILPPDHK _____

Puzzle 10-28 *answers on page 277*

DJT KCT ZTMG FJ QCSSG OQJT BQJG NZ

_____

TZB CXXADJ BQCB BQJ ZFVJKB ZE

_____

MPEJ PX QCSSPTJXX.

_____

—HJZUHJ ZUOJMM _____

HINTS

Puzzle 10-1: The word "problem" is found in this puzzle.

Puzzle 10-2: The word "child" is found in this puzzle.

Puzzle 10-3: The word "steal" is found in this puzzle.

Puzzle 10-4: The word "good" is found in this puzzle.

Puzzle 10-5: The word "exist" is found in this puzzle.

Puzzle 10-6: The word "doubt" is found in this puzzle.

Puzzle 10-7: The word "solely" is found in this puzzle.

Puzzle 10-8: The word "destroy" is found in this puzzle.

Puzzle 10-9: The word "peace" is found in this puzzle.

Puzzle 10-10: The word "words" is found in this puzzle.

Puzzle 10-11: The word "three" is found in this puzzle.

Puzzle 10-12: The word "kill" is found in this puzzle.

Puzzle 10-13: The word "fools" is found in this puzzle.

Puzzle 10-14: The word "cheer" is found in this puzzle.

Puzzle 10-15: The word "amazing" is found in this puzzle.

Puzzle 10-16: The word "insight" is found in this puzzle.

Puzzle 10-17: The word "intended" is found in this puzzle.

Puzzle 10-18: The word "play" is found in this puzzle.

Puzzle 10-19: The word "advise" is found in this puzzle.

Puzzle 10-20: The word "sleep" is found in this puzzle.

Puzzle 10-21: The word "prevent" is found in this puzzle.

Puzzle 10-22: The word "thoughts" is found in this puzzle.

Puzzle 10-23: The word "creativity" is found in this puzzle.

Puzzle 10-24: The word "swifter" is found in this puzzle.

Puzzle 10-25: The word "lightning" is found in this puzzle.

Puzzle 10-26: The word "fools" is found in this puzzle.

Puzzle 10-27: The word "illiterate" is found in this puzzle.

Puzzle 10-28: The word "object" is found in this puzzle.

Answers

CHAPTER 2: HOLIDAY CELEBRATIONS

Puzzle 2-1

A diplomat is a man who always remembers a woman's birthday but never remembers her age. —Robert Frost

Puzzle 2-2

Birthdays are good for you. Statistics show that the people who have the most live the longest. —Larry Lorenzoni

Puzzle 2-3

Real birthdays are not annual affairs. Real birthdays are the days when we have a new birth. —Ralph Parlette

Puzzle 2-4

Why is a birthday cake the only food you can blow on and spit on and everybody rushes to get a piece? —Bobby Kelton

Puzzle 2-5

I stopped believing in Santa Claus when I was six. Mother took me to see him in a department store and he asked for my autograph. —Shirley Temple

Puzzle 2-6

Christ was born in the first century, yet He belongs to all

centuries. He was born a Jew, yet He belongs to all races. He was born in Bethlehem, yet He belongs to all countries. —George W. Truett

Puzzle 2-7

Christmas is not a time nor a season, but a state of mind. To cherish peace and goodwill, to be plenteous in mercy, is to have the real spirit of Christmas. —Calvin Coolidge

Puzzle 2-8

Let us remember that the Christmas heart is a giving heart, a wide open heart that thinks of others first. —George Matthew Adams

Puzzle 2-9

The magi, as you know, were wise men—wonderfully wise men who brought gifts to the Babe in the manger. They invented the art of giving Christmas presents. —O. Henry

Puzzle 2-10

Christmas is the season for kindling the fire of hospitality in the hall, the genial flame of charity in the heart. —Washington Irving

Puzzle 2-11

Frosty the snowman was a jolly happy soul, With a corncob pipe and a button nose, and two eyes made out of coal.

Puzzle 2-12

Jingle bells, jingle bells, jingle all the way,
Oh what fun it is to ride in a one-horse open sleigh.

Puzzle 2-13

Rudolph the red-nosed reindeer had a very shiny nose,
And if you ever saw it, you would even say it glows.

Puzzle 2-14

On the first day of Christmas,
My true love gave to me:
A partridge in a pear tree.

Puzzle 2-15

'Tis now the very witching time of night,
When churchyards yawn and hell itself breathes out Contagion to this world.
—William Shakespeare

Puzzle 2-16

From ghoulies to ghosties and long-leggety beasties and things that go bump in the night, Good Lord, deliver us!
—Author Unknown

Puzzle 2-17

Drop the last year into the silent limbo of the past. Let it go, for it was imperfect, and thank God that it can go.
—Brooks Atkinson

Puzzle 2-18

Each age has deemed the new-born year
The fittest time for festal cheer. —Sir Walter Scott

Puzzle 2-19

The Pilgrims made seven times more graves than huts. No Americans have been more impoverished than these who, nevertheless, set aside a day of thanksgiving. —H. U. Westermayer

Puzzle 2-20

Thanksgiving Day is a jewel, to set in the hearts of honest men; but be careful that you do not take the day, and leave out the gratitude. —E. P. Powell

Puzzle 2-21

True thanksgiving means that we need to thank God for what He has done for us, and not to tell Him what we have done for Him. —George R. Hendrick

CHAPTER 3: LAUGHING OUT LOUD

Puzzle 3-1

How can I believe in God when just last week I got my tongue caught in the roller of an electric typewriter?

Puzzle 3-2

I'm astounded by people who want to "know" the universe when it's hard enough to find your way around Chinatown.

Puzzle 3-3

Organized crime in America takes in over forty billion dollars a year and spends very little on office supplies.

Puzzle 3-4

When the Academy called, I panicked. I thought they might want their Oscars back and the pawn shop has been out of business for awhile.

Puzzle 3-5

I was thrown out of college for cheating on the metaphysics exam; I looked into the soul of the boy sitting next to me.

Puzzle 3-6

I regret the passing of the studio system. I was very appreciative of it because I had no talent.

Puzzle 3-7

I think knowing what you cannot do is more important than knowing what you can do. In fact, that's good taste.

Puzzle 3-8

If you want something done, ask a busy person to do it. The more things you do, the more you can do.

Puzzle 3-9

One of the things I learned the hard way was that it doesn't pay to get discouraged.

Puzzle 3-10

A man who correctly guesses a woman's age may be smart, but he's not very bright.

Puzzle 3-11

Women's Lib? . . . It doesn't interest me one bit. I've been so liberated it hurts.

Puzzle 3-12

I don't believe in dying. It's been done. I'm working on a new exit. Besides, I can't die now—I'm booked.

Puzzle 3-13

The most important thing in acting is honesty. If you can fake that, you've got it made.

Puzzle 3-14

Too bad all the people who know how to run this country are busy running taxicabs or cutting hair.

Puzzle 3-15

Smartness runs in my family. When I went to school I was so smart my teacher was in my class for five years.

Puzzle 3-16

I can't understand why I flunked American history. When I was a kid there was so little of it.

Puzzle 3-17

Human beings are the only creatures that allow their children to come back home.

Puzzle 3-18

The very first law in advertising is to avoid the concrete promise and cultivate the delightfully vague.

Puzzle 3-19

I don't know the key to success, but the key to failure is trying to please everybody.

Puzzle 3-20

Like everyone else who makes the mistake of getting older, I begin each day with coffee and obituaries.

Puzzle 3-21

A word to the wise ain't necessary—it's the stupid ones that need the advice.

Puzzle 3-22

The truth is that parents are not really interested in justice. They just want quiet.

Puzzle 3-23

First the doctor told me the good news: I was going to have a disease named after me.

Puzzle 3-24

Boy, those French, they have a different word for everything!

Puzzle 3-25

I believe that sex is the most beautiful, natural, and wholesome thing that money can buy.

Puzzle 3-26

I like a woman with a head on her shoulders. I hate necks.

Puzzle 3-27

Chaos in the midst of chaos isn't funny, but chaos in the midst of order is.

Puzzle 3-28

I think I did pretty well, considering I started out with nothing but a bunch of blank paper.

Puzzle 3-29

I believe entertainment can aspire to be art, and can become art, but if you set out to make art you're an idiot.

CHAPTER 4: GET INSPIRED

Puzzle 4-1

It is a mistake to try to look too far ahead. The chain of destiny can only be grasped one link at a time.

Puzzle 4-2

We make a living by what we get, we make a life by what we give.

Puzzle 4-3

We shall not fail or falter; we shall not weaken or tire . . . Give us the tools and we will finish the job.

Puzzle 4-4

Now this is not the end. It is not even the beginning of the end. But it is, perhaps, the end of the beginning.

Puzzle 4-5

You cannot do a kindness too soon because you never know how soon it will be too late.

Puzzle 4-6

What lies behind us and what lies before us are small matters compared to what lies within us.

Puzzle 4-7

Don't be too timid and squea-mish about your actions. All life is an experiment. The more experiments you make the better.

Puzzle 4-8

The difference between what we do and what we are capa-ble of doing would suffice to solve most of the world's problems.

Puzzle 4-9

To forgive is not to forget. The merit lies in loving in spite of the vivid knowledge that the one that must be loved is not a friend.

Puzzle 4-10

I have nothing new to teach the world. Truth and Non-violence are as old as the hills. All I have done is to try experiments in both on as vast a scale as I could.

Puzzle 4-11

All progress is precarious, and the solution of one prob-lem brings us face to face with another problem.

Puzzle 4-12

I believe that unarmed truth and unconditional love will have the final word in reality. That is why right, temporarily defeated, is stronger than evil triumphant.

Puzzle 4-13

The ultimate measure of a man is not where he stands in moments of comfort and convenience, but where he stands at times of challenge and controversy.

Puzzle 4-14

Everybody today seems to be in such a terrible rush; anxious for greater developments and greater wishes and so on; so that children have very little time for their parents.

Puzzle 4-15

It is not how much we do, but how much love we put in the doing. It is not how much we give, but how much love we put in the giving.

Puzzle 4-16

Do not think that love, in order to be genuine, has to be extraordinary. What we need is to love without getting tired.

Puzzle 4-17

If you hear a voice within you say "You cannot paint," then by all means paint, and that voice will be silenced. —Vincent Van Gogh

Puzzle 4-18

Let every man or woman here, if you never hear me again, remember this, that if you wish to be great at all, you must begin where you are and with what you are. He who would be great anywhere must first be great in his own Philadelphia. —Russell H. Conwell

Puzzle 4-19

Use what talent you possess: the woods would be very silent if no birds sang except those that sang best. —Henry Van Dyke

Puzzle 4-20

Here is a test to find out whether your mission in life is complete. If you're alive, it isn't. —Richard Bach

Puzzle 4-21

Most of the important things in the world have been accomplished by people who have kept on trying when there seemed to be no hope at all. —Dale Carnegie

Puzzle 4-22

We simply assume that the way we see things is the way they really are or the way they should be. And our attitudes and behaviors grow out of these assumptions. —Steven Covey

CHAPTER 5: GOING TO THE MOVIES

Puzzle 5-1

In films murders are always very clean. I show how difficult it is and what a messy thing it is to kill a man. —Alfred Hitchcock

Puzzle 5-2

I've been failing for, like, ten or eleven years. When it turns, it'll turn. Right now I'm just tryin' to squeeze through a very tight financial period, get the movie out, and put my things in order.

—Francis Ford Coppola

Puzzle 5-3

To grasp the full significance of life is the actor's duty, to interpret it is his problem, and to express it his dedication.

—Marlon Brando

Puzzle 5-4

My films are the expression of momentary desires. I follow my instincts, but in a disciplined way. —Roman Polanski

Puzzle 5-5

My dentist said to me the other day, I've enough problems in my life, so why should I see your films? —David Cronenberg

Puzzle 5-6

A man who tells lies, like me, merely hides the truth. But a man who tells half-lies has forgotten where he put it.

—Claude Rains

Puzzle 5-7

You can break a man's skull. You can arrest him. You can throw him into a dungeon. But how do you fight an idea?

—Andre Morell

Puzzle 5-8

I think now, looking back, we did not fight the enemy, we fought ourselves. The enemy was in us. The war is over for me now, but it will always be there, the rest of my days.
—Charlie Sheen

Puzzle 5-9

Yeah, but your scientists were so preoccupied with whether or not they could, they didn't stop to think if they should.
—Jeff Goldblum

Puzzle 5-10

I will tell you of William Wallace. Historians will call me a liar, but history is written by those who've hanged heroes.
—Angus MacFayden

Puzzle 5-11

To be my own master, such a thing would be greater than all the treasure and all the magic in the world. —Robin Williams

Puzzle 5-12

The flower that blooms in adversity is the rarest and most beautiful of all.
—Pat Morita

Puzzle 5-13

Most everyone's mad here. You may have noticed that I'm not all there myself.
—Sterling Holloway

Puzzle 5-14

I'm from Mattel. Well, actually I'm from a smaller company

that was purchased by Mattel in a leveraged buyout. —Wallace Shawn

Puzzle 5-15

Simba, let me tell you something my father told me. Look at the stars, the great kings of the past are up there, watching over us. —James Earl Jones

Puzzle 5-16

I can't think about that right now. If I do, I'll go crazy. I'll think about that tomorrow. —Vivien Leigh

Puzzle 5-17

A normal human being couldn't live under the same roof with her without going nutty! —Clark Gable

Puzzle 5-18

You see, George, you've really had a wonderful life. Don't you see what a mistake it would be to just throw it away? —Henry Travers

Puzzle 5-19

You see, boys forget what their country means by just reading The Land of the Free in history books. —James Stewart

Puzzle 5-20

I've got to do something about the way I look. I mean, a girl just can't go to Sing Sing with a green face. —Audrey Hepburn

Puzzle 5-21

Life is like a box of chocolates. You never know what you're going to get. —Tom Hanks

Puzzle 5-22

Good morning! And in case I don't see you: good afternoon, good evening, and good night! —Jim Carrey

Puzzle 5-23

The new phone book's here! The new phone book's here! This is the kind of spontaneous publicity I need! My name in print! That really makes somebody! Things are going to start happening to me now. —Steve Martin

Puzzle 5-24

You treat a disease—you win, you lose. But I guarantee, you treat a person and you win no matter the outcome. —Robin Williams

Puzzle 5-25

Elaine, you're a member of this crew. Can you face some unpleasant facts? —Leslie Nielsen

Puzzle 5-26

I can't believe you're a professional golfer. I think you should be working at the snack bar. —Bob Barker

Puzzle 5-27

Destiny is something we've invented because we can't stand the fact that everything that happens is accidental. —Meg Ryan

Puzzle 5-28

You've gotta win a little, lose a little,
and always have the blues just a little;
That's the story of, the glory of love. —Bette Midler

Puzzle 5-29

I would rather have thirty minutes of wonderful than a lifetime of nothing special. —Julia Roberts

Puzzle 5-30

People fall in love. They fall right back out. It happens all the time. —Sandra Bullock

Puzzle 5-31

I came here tonight because when you realize you want to spend the rest of your life with somebody, you want the rest of your life to start as soon as possible. —Billy Crystal

Puzzle 5-32

I would rather have had one breath of her hair, one kiss from her mouth, one touch of her hand, than eternity without it. —Nicolas Cage

Puzzle 5-33

Make of our hands one hand.
Make of our hearts one heart.
Make of our vows one last
vow. Only death will part us
now —Richard Beymer

Puzzle 5-34

In every job that must be
done, there is an element of
fun. You find the fun and—
SNAP—the job's a game.
—Julie Andrews

Puzzle 5-35

If you want to view paradise,
simply look around and view
it. Anything you want to, do
it. Want to change the world?
There's nothing to it. —Gene
Wilder

Puzzle 5-36

First she steals my publicity.
Then she steals my lawyer,
my trial date. And now she
steals my goddamn garter.
—Catherine Zeta-Jones

Puzzle 5-37

If I die, I'm sorry for all the bad
things I did to you. And if I live,
I'm sorry for all the bad things
I'm gonna do to you. —Roy
Scheider

Puzzle 5-38

If we bring a little joy into your
humdrum lives, it makes us
feel as if our hard work ain't
been in vain for nothing.
—Jean Hagen

Puzzle 5-39

There was love all around, but I never heard it singing. No I never heard it at all, till there was you. —Shirley Jones

CHAPTER 6: IT'S ALL POLITICS

Puzzle 6-1

O how small a portion of earth will hold us when we are dead, who ambitiously seek after the whole world while we are living. —Philip II

Puzzle 6-2

No more tears now; I will think upon revenge.
—Mary Queen of Scots

Puzzle 6-3

All strange and terrible events are welcome, but comforts we despise. —Cleopatra

Puzzle 6-4

It is necessary to try to surpass oneself always; this occupation ought to last as long as life. —Queen Christina

Puzzle 6-5

I have found it impossible to carry the heavy burden of responsibility . . . —King Edward VIII

Puzzle 6-6

The whole world is in revolt. Soon there will be only five Kings left—the King of England, the King of Spades, the

King of Clubs, the King of Hearts, and the King of Diamonds. —King Farouk

Puzzle 6-7

Democratic nations must try to find ways to starve the terrorist and the hijacker of the oxygen of publicity on which they depend. —Margaret Thatcher

Puzzle 6-8

Power without principle is barren, but principle without power is futile. This is a party of government, and I will lead it as a party of government. —Tony Blair

Puzzle 6-9

There is one common factor that should be essential to whatever Parliamentary reforms are suggested . . . the need for greater recognition of the crucial role of the individual Member of Parliament. —Paul Martin

Puzzle 6-10

I don't think there's any reason on Earth why people should have access to automatic and semiautomatic weapons unless they're in the military or in the police. —John Howard

Puzzle 6-11

We have not eternal allies and we have not perpetual enemies. Our interests are eternal and perpetual and those interests it is our duty to follow. —Lord Palmerston

Puzzle 6-12

A decent and manly examination of the acts of government should not only be tolerated, but encouraged. —William Harrison

Puzzle 6-13

The policy of the American government is to leave their citizens free, neither restraining nor aiding them in their pursuits. —Thomas Jefferson

Puzzle 6-14

Government is not reason; it is not eloquent; it is force. Like fire, it is a dangerous servant and a fearful master. —George Washington

Puzzle 6-15

And so, my fellow Americans: ask not what your country can do for you—ask what you can do for your country. —John F. Kennedy

Puzzle 6-16

Government must keep pace with the changing needs of our state and its people to be sure that government can fulfill its legitimate obligations. —Ronald Reagan

Puzzle 6-17

We're all capable of mistakes, but I do not care to enlighten you on the mistakes we may or may not have made. —George W. Bush

Puzzle 6-18

When the President does it, that means that it's not illegal. —Richard Nixon

Puzzle 6-19

Politics is not a bad profession. If you succeed there are many rewards, if you disgrace yourself you can always write a book. —Ronald Reagan

Puzzle 6-20

I like the job. That's what I'll miss the most . . . I'm not sure anybody ever liked this as much as I've liked it. —Bill Clinton

Puzzle 6-21

We have a firm commitment to NATO, we are a part of NATO. We have a firm commitment to Europe, we are a part of Europe. —George W. Bush

Puzzle 6-22

No matter how hard the loss, defeat might serve as well as victory to shake the soul and let the glory out. —Al Gore

Puzzle 6-23

I have made good judgments in the past. I have made good judgments in the future. —Dan Quayle

Puzzle 6-24

For the first time in the history of mankind, one generation literally has the power to destroy the past, the present, and the future, the power to bring time to an end. —Hubert H. Humphrey

Puzzle 6-25

Confronted with the choice, the American people would choose the policeman's truncheon over the anarchist's bomb. —Spiro T. Agnew

Puzzle 6-26

It is essential that we enable young people to see themselves as participants in one of the most exciting eras in history, and to have a sense of purpose in relation to it. —Nelson Rockefeller

Puzzle 6-27

Ideas are far more powerful than guns. We don't allow our enemies to have guns, why should we allow them to have ideas? —Josef Stalin

Puzzle 6-28

I would rather excel others in the knowledge of what is excellent than in the extent of my powers and dominion. —Alexander the Great

Puzzle 6-29

I never did anything alone. Whatever was accomplished in this country was accomplished collectively. —Golda Meir

Puzzle 6-30

There exists no politician in India daring enough to attempt to explain to the masses that cows can be eaten. —Indira Gandhi

CHAPTER 7: RELIGION AND SPIRITUALITY

Puzzle 7-1

I cannot conceive of a God who rewards and punishes his creatures, or has a will of the type of which we are conscious in ourselves. —Albert Einstein

Puzzle 7-2

My deeply held belief is that if a god anything like the traditional sort exists, our curiosity and intelligence are provided by such a god. We would be unappreciative of those

gifts . . . if we suppressed our passion to explore the universe and ourselves. —Carl Sagan

Puzzle 7-3

Many people genuinely do not wish to be saints, and it is possible that some who achieve or aspire to sainthood have never had much temptation to be human beings. —George Orwell

Puzzle 7-4

God is really only another artist. He invented the giraffe, the elephant, and the cat. He has no real style. He just keeps on trying other things. —Pablo Picasso

Puzzle 7-5

People fashion their God after their own understanding. They make their God first and worship him afterwards. —Oscar Wilde

Puzzle 7-6

To have a positive religion is not necessary. To be in harmony with yourself and the universe is what counts, and this is possible without positive and specific formulation in words. —Johann Wolfgang von Goethe

Puzzle 7-7

An idea that is developed and put into action is more important than an idea that exists only as an idea.

Puzzle 7-8

Do not overrate what you have received, nor envy others. He who envies others does not obtain peace of mind.

Puzzle 7-9

To be idle is a short road to death and to be diligent is a way of life; foolish people are idle, wise people are diligent.

Puzzle 7-10

Words have the power to both destroy and heal. When words are both true and kind, they can change our world.

Puzzle 7-11

If you knew what I know about the power of giving, you would not let a single meal pass without sharing it in some way.

Puzzle 7-12

Let yourself be open and life will be easier. A spoon of salt in a glass of water makes the water undrinkable. A spoon of salt in a lake is almost unnoticed.

Puzzle 7-13

Holding on to anger is like grasping a hot coal with the intent of throwing it at some-one else; you are the one who gets burned.

Puzzle 7-14

The man of virtue makes the difficulty to be overcome his first business, and suc-cess only a subsequent consideration.

Puzzle 7-15

I have not seen a person who loved virtue, or one who hated what was not virtuous. He who loved virtue would esteem nothing above it.

Puzzle 7-16

Our greatest glory consists not in never falling, but in rising every time we fall.

Puzzle 7-17

What you do not want done to yourself, do not do to others.

Puzzle 7-18

When we see men of worth, we should think of equaling them; when we see men of a contrary character, we should turn inwards and examine ourselves.

Puzzle 7-19

Listen to all the teachers in the woods. Watch the trees, the animals and all the living things—you'll learn more from them than books. —Joe Coyhis

Puzzle 7-20

A very great vision is needed and the man who has it must follow it as the eagle seeks the deepest blue of the sky. —Crazy Horse

Puzzle 7-21

The Great Spirit Chief who rules above all will smile upon this land . . . and this time the Indian race is waiting and praying.—Chief Joseph

Puzzle 7-22

All things share the same breath—the beast, the tree, the man, the air shares its spirit with all the life it supports. —Chief Seattle

Puzzle 7-23

Like the grasses showing tender faces to each other, thus should we do, for this was the wish of the Grandfathers of the World. —Black Elk

Puzzle 7-24

Let your light shine before men, that they may see your

good works, and glorify your Father which is in heaven.

Puzzle 7-25

Do not forget to entertain strangers, for by so doing some have unwittingly entertained angels.

Puzzle 7-26

Therefore we do not lose heart. Even though our outward man is perishing, yet the inward man is being renewed day by day.

Puzzle 7-27

Foolishness is bound in the heart of a child; but the rod of correction shall drive it far from him.

Puzzle 7-28

There is nothing better for a man, than that he should eat and drink, and that he should make his soul enjoy good in his labor.

Puzzle 7-29

Husbands, love your wives, just as Christ also loved the church and gave himself up for her.

Puzzle 7-30

His is the kingdom of the heavens and the earth. He ordains life and death and has power over all things.

Puzzle 7-31

Attend constantly to prayers and to the middle prayer and

stand up truly obedient to Allah.

Puzzle 7-32

We have made you a just nation, so that you may testify against mankind and that your own Apostle may testify against you.

Puzzle 7-33

The seven heavens, the earth, and all who dwell in them give glory to Him. All creatures celebrate His praises. Yet you cannot understand their praises. Benignant is He and forgiving.

Puzzle 7-34

Prayer carries us half way to God, fasting brings us to the door of His palace, and alms-giving procures us admission.

Puzzle 7-35

A dream which is not interpreted is like a letter which is not read.

Puzzle 7-36

Who forces time is pushed back by time; who yields to time, finds time on his side.

Puzzle 7-37

Whoever destroys a single life is as guilty as though he had destroyed the entire world; and whoever rescues a single life earns as much merit as though he had rescued the entire world.

CHAPTER 8: SCIENTIFIC DISCOVERIES

Puzzle 8-1

In the survival of favored individuals and races, during the constantly-recurring struggle for existence, we see a powerful and ever-acting form of selection. —Charles Darwin

Puzzle 8-2

Science has proof without any certainty. Creationists have certainty without any proof. —Ashley Montague

Puzzle 8-3

The essence of life is statistical improbability on a colossal scale. —Richard Dawkins

Puzzle 8-4

I have called this principle, by which each slight variation, if useful, is preserved, by the term Natural Selection. —Charles Darwin

Puzzle 8-5

In every outthrust headland, in every curving beach, in every grain of sand there is a story of the earth. —Rachel Carson

Puzzle 8-6

I recently read that love is entirely a matter of chemistry. That must be why my wife treats me like toxic waste. —David Bissonette

Puzzle 8-7

Let me tell you the secret that has led me to my goal: my strength lies solely in my tenacity. —Louis Pasteur

Puzzle 8-8

All theoretical chemistry is really physics; and all theoretical chemists know it.
—Richard P. Feynman

Puzzle 8-9

I was taught that the way of progress is neither swift nor easy. —Marie Curie

Puzzle 8-10

Organic chemistry is the chemistry of carbon compounds. Biochemistry is the study of carbon compounds that crawl. —Mike Adams

Puzzle 8-11

The definition of insanity is doing the same thing over and over and expecting different results. —Benjamin Franklin

Puzzle 8-12

There is nothing in a caterpillar that tells you it's going to be a butterfly. —Richard Buckminster Fuller

Puzzle 8-13

The human brain must continue to frame the problems for the electronic machine to solve. —David Sarnoff

Puzzle 8-14

An inventor fails nine hundred and ninety-nine times, and if he succeeds once, he's in. He treats his failures simply as practice shots. —Charles F. Kettering

Puzzle 8-15

If we all worked on the assumption that what is accepted as true is really true, there would be little hope of advance. —Orville Wright

Puzzle 8-16

Anything that won't sell, I don't want to invent. Its sale is proof of utility, and utility is success. —Thomas A. Edison

Puzzle 8-17

Mathematics is a game played according to certain simple rules with meaningless marks on paper. —David Hilbert

Puzzle 8-18

Mathematics is the art of giving the same name to different things. —Jules Henri Poincare

Puzzle 8-19

A mathematician's reputation rests on the number of bad proofs he has given. —A. S. Besicovich

Puzzle 8-20

Medicine makes people ill, mathematics make them sad, and theology makes them sinful. —Martin Luther

Puzzle 8-21

What is man in nature? Nothing in relation to the infinite, all in relation to nothing, a mean between nothing and everything. —Blaise Pascal

Puzzle 8-22

There is not the slightest indication that energy will ever be obtainable from the atom.
—Albert Einstein

Puzzle 8-23

If you wish to make an apple pie truly from scratch, you must first invent the universe.
—Carl Sagan

Puzzle 8-24

My goal is simple. It is complete understanding of the universe, why it is as it is and why it exists at all. —Stephen Hawking

Puzzle 8-25

Those who are not shocked when they first come across quantum mechanics cannot possibly have understood it.
—Niels Bohr

Puzzle 8-26

All of physics is either impossible or trivial. It is impossible until you understand it, and then it becomes trivial.
—Ernest Rutherford

Puzzle 8-27

Research is formalized curiosity. It is poking and prying with a purpose. —Zora Neale Hurston

Puzzle 8-28

Physics isn't a religion. If it were, we'd have a much easier time raising money.
—Leon Lederman

Puzzle 8-29

Research is the art of seeing what everyone else has seen, and doing what no one else has done. —Anonymous

Puzzle 8-30

It is a good morning exercise for a research scientist to discard a pet hypothesis every day before breakfast. It keeps him young. —Konrad Lorenz

Puzzle 8-31

The trouble with research is that it tells you what people were thinking about yesterday, not tomorrow. It's like driving a car using a rearview mirror.
—Bernard Loomis

CHAPTER 9: PLAYING SPORTS

Puzzle 9-1

You spend a good piece of your life gripping a baseball, and it turns out it was the other way around all the time.
—Jim Bouton

Puzzle 9-2

If it weren't for baseball, many kids wouldn't know what a millionaire looked like. —Phyllis Diller

Puzzle 9-3

The hardest thing to do in baseball is to hit a round baseball with a round bat, squarely. —Ted Williams

Puzzle 9-4

I never threw an illegal pitch. The trouble is, once in a while I toss one that ain't never been seen by this generation. —Satchel Paige

Puzzle 9-5

I never looked at the consequences of missing a big shot . . . when you think about the consequences you always think of a negative result. —Michael Jordan

Puzzle 9-6

They say that nobody is perfect. Then they tell you practice makes perfect. I wish they'd make up their minds. —Wilt Chamberlain

Puzzle 9-7

Good, better, best. Never let it rest. Until your good is better and your better is best. —Tim Duncan

Puzzle 9-8

Any American boy can be a basketball star if he grows up, up, up. —Bill Vaughn

Puzzle 9-9

I always laugh when people ask me about rebounding techniques. I've got a technique.

It's called just go get the damn ball. —Charles Barkley

Puzzle 9-10

I believe the game is designed to reward the ones who hit the hardest. If you can't take it, you shouldn't play. —Jack Lambert

Puzzle 9-11

Politics is like football; if you see daylight, go through the hole. —John F. Kennedy

Puzzle 9-12

If a man watches three football games in a row, he should be declared legally dead. —Erma Bombeck

Puzzle 9-13

If you can keep your head when all about you are los-

ing theirs, you're at the wrong end of the football pitch. —Bill Munro

Puzzle 9-14

Football brings out the sociologist that lurks in some otherwise respectable citizens. They say football is a metaphor for America's sinfulness. —George F. Will

Puzzle 9-15

Golf is a game in which a ball—one and a half inches in diameter—is placed on a ball—eight thousand miles in diameter. The object being to hit the small ball but not the larger. —John Cunningham

Puzzle 9-16

If you are going to throw a club, it is important to throw it ahead of you, down the fairway, so you don't waste energy going back to pick it up. —Tommy Bolt

Puzzle 9-17

If I'm on the course and lightning starts, I get inside fast. If God wants to play through, let him. —Bob Hope

Puzzle 9-18

I'm in the woods so much I can tell you which plants are edible. —Lee Trevino

Puzzle 9-19

Tee the ball high. Because years of experience have shown me that air offers less resistance than dirt. —Jack Nicklaus

Puzzle 9-20

I had a wonderful experience on the golf course today. I had a hole in nothing. Missed the ball and sank the divot. —Don Adams

Puzzle 9-21

It's not who wins the fight that's important, it's being willing to fight. If you get challenged and renege, everyone wants to take a shot at you. —Barclay Plager

Puzzle 9-22

A puck is a hard rubber disc that hockey players strike

when they can't hit one another. —Jimmy Cannon

Puzzle 9-23

We get nose jobs all the time in the NHL, and we don't even have to go to the hospital.
—Brad Park

Puzzle 9-24

We take the shortest route to the puck and arrive in ill humor. —Bobby Clarke

Puzzle 9-25

A player must be able to skate, have hockey sense, be able to shoot—not necessarily able to score—and have drive.
—Pierre Page

Puzzle 9-26

You've got to take the initiative and play your game. In a decisive set, confidence is the difference. —Chris Evert

Puzzle 9-27

You can almost watch a couple play mixed doubles and know whether they should stay together. —Dr. Herbert Hendin

Puzzle 9-28

The trouble with me is that every match I play against five opponents: umpire, crowd, ball boys, court, and myself.
—Goran Ivanisevic

Puzzle 9-29

An otherwise happily married couple may turn a mixed doubles game into a scene from *Who's Afraid of Virginia Woolf.* —Rod Laver

CHAPTER 10: CRYPTOGRAM JUMBLE

Puzzle 10-1

The problem is not that there are problems. The problem is expecting otherwise and thinking that having problems is a problem. —Theodore Rubin

Puzzle 10-2

Every child is an artist. The problem is how to remain an artist once he grows up. —Pablo Picasso

Puzzle 10-3

Progress always involves risk; you can't steal second base and keep your foot on first base. —Frederick Wilcox

Puzzle 10-4

You're never as good as everyone tells you when you win, and you're never as bad as they say when you lose. —Lou Holtz

Puzzle 10-5

The problems that exist in the world today cannot be solved by the level of thinking that created them. —Albert Einstein

Puzzle 10-6

Never doubt that a small group of thoughtful committed people can change the world: indeed it's the only thing that ever has! —Margaret Meade

Puzzle 10-7

Remember happiness doesn't depend upon who you are or what you have; it depends solely on what you think. —Dale Carnegie

Puzzle 10-8

Always remember, others may hate you. But those who hate you don't win unless you hate them. And then you destroy yourself. —Richard M. Nixon

Puzzle 10-9

I think that people want peace so much that one of these days governments had better get out of the way and let them have it. —Dwight D. Eisenhower

Puzzle 10-10

Kindness in words creates confidence. Kindness in thinking creates profoundness. Kindness in giving creates love. —Lao Tzu

Puzzle 10-11

They say a person needs just three things to be truly happy in this world: someone to love, something to do, and something to hope for. —Tom Bodett

Puzzle 10-12

I am prepared to die, but there is no cause for which I am prepared to kill. —Mahatma Gandhi

Puzzle 10-13

Wise men talk because they have something to say; fools, because they have to say something. —Plato

Puzzle 10-14

The best way to cheer yourself is to try to cheer someone else up. —Mark Twain

Puzzle 10-15

When you have confidence, you can have a lot of fun. And when you have fun, you can do amazing things. —Joe Namath

Puzzle 10-16

If one is master of one thing and understands one thing well, one has at the same time, insight into and understanding of many things. —Vincent van Gogh

Puzzle 10-17

I may not have gone where I intended to go, but I think I have ended up where I intended to be. —Douglas Adams

Puzzle 10-18

You can discover more about a person in an hour of play than in a year of conversation. —Plato

Puzzle 10-19

I have found the best way to give advice to your children is to find out what they want and then advise them to do it. —Harry S. Truman

Puzzle 10-20

The good people sleep much better at night than the bad people. Of course, the bad people enjoy the waking hours much more. —Woody Allen

Puzzle 10-21

Today the real test of power is not capacity to make war but the capacity to prevent it. —Anne O'Hare McCormick

Puzzle 10-22

We are shaped by our thoughts; we become what we think. When the mind is pure, joy follows like a shadow that never leaves. —Buddha

Puzzle 10-23

Thinking is the enemy of creativity. It's self-conscious, and anything self-conscious is lousy. You can't try to do things. You simply must do things. —Ray Bradbury

Puzzle 10-24

Our progress as a nation can be no swifter than our progress in education. The human mind is our fundamental resource. —John F. Kennedy

Puzzle 10-25

The difference between the right word and the almost right word is the difference between lightning and a lightning bug.
—Mark Twain

Puzzle 10-26

A common mistake that people make when trying to design something completely foolproof is to underestimate the ingenuity of complete fools.
—Douglas Adams

Puzzle 10-27

The illiterate of the future will not be the person who cannot read. It will be the person who does not know how to learn.
—Alvin Toffler

Puzzle 10-28

Men can only be happy when they do not assume that the object of life is happiness.
—George Orwell

We Have EVERYTHING® on Anything!

With more than 19 million copies sold, the Everything® series has become one of America's favorite resources for solving problems, learning new skills, and organizing lives. Our brand is not only recognizable—it's also welcomed.

The series is a hand-in-hand partner for people who are ready to tackle new subjects—like you!

For more information on the Everything® series, please visit *www.adamsmedia.com*

The Everything® list spans a wide range of subjects, with more than 500 titles covering 25 different categories:

Business	History	Reference
Careers	Home Improvement	Religion
Children's Storybooks	Everything Kids	Self-Help
Computers	Languages	Sports & Fitness
Cooking	Music	Travel
Crafts and Hobbies	New Age	Wedding
Education/Schools	Parenting	Writing
Games and Puzzles	Personal Finance	
Health	Pets	